Using SBA Mortgage Loans for Construction and Expansion

How to Build, Renovate, or Expand Commercial Properties with SBA Financing

By Joseph G. Correa

Licensed Mortgage Broker, Finibi Mortgage

Copyright & Legal Notice

Published by Live Stronger Faster

analysis, property acquisition, refinancing, construction financing, and advanced loan structuring. These examples do not represent guaranteed approvals, loan terms, or outcomes. Results may vary significantly based on individual financial profiles, credit history, business performance, property type, market conditions, and lender-specific guidelines.

SBA loan programs are subject to eligibility requirements, regulatory guidelines, and changes established by the U.S. Small Business Administration and participating lenders. Borrowers are encouraged to consult directly with qualified financial, legal, and tax professionals before making any financing or investment decisions.

The author and publisher make no representations or warranties regarding the accuracy, completeness, or applicability of the content and disclaim any liability for errors, omissions, or outcomes resulting from the use or misuse of the information contained in this book.

All trademarks, service marks, company names, and product names referenced in this publication are the property of their respective owners and are used strictly for identification and educational purposes only. Their inclusion does not imply endorsement or affiliation.

First Edition, 2026

Table of Contents

Introduction

In the world of commercial real estate and business growth, there comes a point when acquisition is no longer enough. Ownership is only the beginning. The true transformation happens when you build, expand, renovate, and reposition your property or business to unlock higher income, stronger equity, and long-term scalability. This is where construction and expansion financing becomes one of the most powerful tools available to entrepreneurs and investors. Yet for many borrowers, construction financing feels complex, risky, and difficult to access. Traditional lenders often impose strict requirements, large down payments, and limited flexibility, making it challenging for small business owners to execute their vision. This is precisely where programs backed by the U.S. Small Business Administration step in to create opportunity.

SBA mortgage programs are not just for purchasing existing properties—they are designed to help you build from the ground up, renovate outdated structures, expand your current operations, and create entirely new income-producing assets. Whether you are constructing a new office building, expanding a medical practice, developing a warehouse, or upgrading a retail space, SBA construction and expansion loans offer unique advantages that traditional financing cannot match. These include lower down payments, longer repayment terms, competitive interest rates, and the ability to finance both real estate and business operations under one strategic structure. For entrepreneurs who understand how to leverage these programs, SBA construction financing becomes a pathway to accelerated growth and long-term wealth creation.

One of the most important shifts in mindset that this book will help you develop is the understanding that construction is not just about building structures—it is about building value. Every square foot you add, every improvement you make, and every expansion you execute has the potential to increase revenue, improve efficiency, and strengthen your market position. SBA financing allows you to align your physical expansion with your business strategy, ensuring that your growth is not limited by capital constraints. Instead of waiting years to accumulate the funds needed for expansion, you can move forward now with a structured financing plan that supports your vision.

Construction projects, however, come with a unique set of challenges. Unlike purchasing an existing property, where value and condition are already established, construction involves uncertainty. Costs can fluctuate, timelines can shift, and unforeseen issues can arise. Lenders recognize these risks, which is why construction financing requires detailed planning, strong documentation, and a clear execution strategy. In this book, you will learn how SBA lenders evaluate construction deals, what documentation is required, how budgets are structured, and how to present your project in a way that maximizes your chances of approval. You will also learn how to anticipate and manage risks so that your project stays on track from start to finish.

A key advantage of SBA construction loans is their flexibility. Through programs such as SBA 7(a) and SBA 504, borrowers can finance a wide range of projects, including ground-up construction, major renovations, property expansions, and even improvements to existing facilities. These programs can also include soft costs such as architectural fees, permits, engineering, and contingency reserves, which are often overlooked but critical to the success of any construction project. By understanding how to structure these components properly, you can ensure that your financing covers not just the visible costs, but the full scope of your development.

Another powerful aspect of SBA construction financing is its alignment with owner-occupied business models. Unlike many traditional commercial loans that focus heavily on investment properties, SBA programs are specifically designed to support businesses that occupy and operate within their properties.

This creates a unique opportunity for business owners to build equity while simultaneously growing their operations. Instead of paying rent to a landlord, you are investing in your own asset, increasing its value, and creating a long-term foundation for your business. Over time, this strategy can significantly enhance your net worth and financial stability.

Throughout this book, you will also discover how construction financing can be used strategically to scale your business. Expansion is not just about adding space—it is about increasing capacity, improving efficiency, and positioning your business for future growth. Whether you are adding new locations, expanding your current facility, or upgrading your infrastructure, SBA financing allows you to execute these moves with confidence. You will learn how to evaluate when expansion makes sense, how to structure your project for maximum return on investment, and how to align your financing with your long-term goals.

Another critical element covered in this book is the construction process itself from a lender's perspective. SBA lenders require detailed project plans, including timelines, budgets, contractor agreements, and feasibility analysis. They want to see that your project is not only viable but also well-managed. This means working with experienced professionals such as general contractors, architects, and engineers who can bring your vision to life while maintaining financial discipline. You will learn how to assemble the right team, how to present your project professionally, and how to navigate the approval process with clarity and confidence.

In addition to approval, managing the construction phase is equally important. SBA construction loans are typically disbursed through a draw process, where funds are released in stages as the project progresses. Understanding how this process works is essential to maintaining cash flow and ensuring that your project stays on schedule. You will learn how to coordinate with your lender, manage draw requests, and avoid common pitfalls that can delay funding or disrupt your timeline. Proper management during this phase can make the difference between a successful project and a costly setback.

This book will also explore the long-term benefits of construction and expansion through SBA financing. Beyond the immediate impact of completing your project, these investments can significantly increase your property's value, enhance your business operations, and create new revenue streams. For example, expanding a facility may allow you to serve more customers, introduce new services, or improve operational efficiency. Renovating a property can attract higher-paying tenants or customers, while building from the ground up allows you to design a space that perfectly aligns with your business needs. Each of these outcomes contributes to a stronger, more resilient financial future. As you move through this book, you will begin to see construction financing not as a complex obstacle, but as a strategic opportunity. The key is understanding how to structure your deal, present your project, and execute your plan effectively. SBA programs are designed to support your growth, but they require preparation, discipline, and a clear vision. By mastering these elements, you can transform your ideas into tangible assets that generate income and build wealth over time.

Ultimately, this book is about empowering you to take control of your expansion. Whether you are a business owner looking to grow your operations, an investor seeking to develop new properties, or an entrepreneur ready to build something from the ground up, SBA construction financing provides the tools you need to succeed. With the right knowledge and strategy, you can overcome the barriers that hold most people back and position yourself for long-term success.

The journey of building, renovating, and expanding is one of the most rewarding paths in business and real estate. It requires vision, courage, and execution. But with the support of SBA financing and the strategies outlined in this book, you will be equipped to move forward with confidence. This is where your growth accelerates, your opportunities expand, and your future begins to take shape—not just as an idea, but as a reality you have built with intention and strategy.

Chapter 1

Understanding SBA Construction and Expansion Mortgage Loans

The ability to build, expand, or renovate a commercial property is one of the most powerful wealth-building strategies available to business owners and real estate investors. While purchasing an existing property provides immediate functionality, construction and expansion unlock the next level of control, customization, and long-term profitability. Through SBA-backed mortgage programs supported by the U.S. Small Business Administration, borrowers gain access to financing solutions specifically designed to support growth—not just ownership. These programs allow you to fund projects that transform underutilized land into income-producing assets, convert outdated properties into modern, high-performing spaces, and expand operations to meet increasing demand. Understanding how these loans work is the foundation for executing successful projects and maximizing your return on investment.

SBA construction and expansion mortgage loans are fundamentally different from traditional commercial construction loans. Conventional lenders often require large down payments, short-term financing structures, and strict underwriting criteria that limit flexibility. In contrast, SBA programs such as the 7(a) and 504 loans are designed to encourage small business growth by reducing barriers to entry. These programs allow borrowers to finance not only the hard costs of construction—such as materials and labor—but also soft costs, including architectural design, engineering, permits, and contingency reserves. This comprehensive approach ensures that projects are fully funded from start to finish, reducing the risk of delays or budget shortfalls that could jeopardize completion.

One of the defining features of SBA construction loans is their long-term amortization. Instead of short-term, interest-only construction financing followed by refinancing, many SBA structures allow you to roll construction and permanent financing into a single loan. This eliminates the uncertainty of needing to refinance after completion and provides predictable, long-term payments that align with your business's cash flow. For business owners, this stability is critical. It allows you to focus on operations and growth rather than worrying about future financing risks. This structure also enhances affordability, as payments are spread out over a longer period, making it easier to manage debt while investing in expansion.

Another key advantage is the lower down payment requirement. Traditional construction loans often require 20% to 30% equity, which can be a significant barrier for many borrowers. SBA programs, however, may allow down payments as low as 10%, depending on the structure of the deal and the borrower's qualifications. This lower equity requirement enables you to preserve capital for other critical areas of your business, such as hiring staff, purchasing equipment, or funding marketing efforts. By leveraging SBA financing, you can achieve growth without depleting your cash reserves, creating a more balanced and sustainable financial strategy.

Eligibility for SBA construction loans is centered around the concept of owner occupancy. In most cases, the business must occupy at least 51% of the property for existing buildings or 60% for new construction. This requirement aligns the financing with the SBA's mission of supporting operating businesses rather than purely passive investments. However, this does not limit your ability to generate additional income from the property. You can still lease out unused space, creating supplemental revenue streams that enhance your overall return. This hybrid model—combining business operations with real estate income—is one of the most powerful strategies for building long-term wealth.

Understanding the types of projects that qualify for SBA construction financing is essential. These loans can be used for ground-up construction, major renovations, property expansions, and even improvements to existing facilities. For example, a medical practice might use SBA financing to build a new clinic, while a manufacturing company might expand its warehouse to increase production capacity. A retail business could renovate its storefront to attract more customers, and a service-based business might build a new headquarters to support growth. Each of these scenarios demonstrates how construction financing can be tailored to meet specific business needs.

The underwriting process for SBA construction loans is detailed and thorough, reflecting the complexity and risk associated with construction projects. Lenders evaluate not only the borrower's financial strength but also the feasibility of the project itself. This includes reviewing construction plans, budgets, timelines, contractor qualifications, and market conditions. The goal is to ensure that the project is viable and that the borrower has the capacity to complete it successfully. While this process may seem intensive, it ultimately protects both the borrower and the lender by reducing the likelihood of project failure.

A critical component of SBA construction financing is the budget. A well-structured budget includes both hard and soft costs, as well as a contingency reserve to account for unexpected expenses. Construction projects rarely go exactly as planned, and having a financial cushion is essential to maintaining progress. Lenders typically require a contingency of 5% to 10% of the total project cost, ensuring that you are prepared for unforeseen challenges. By planning for these variables upfront, you can avoid disruptions and keep your project on schedule.

Another important aspect is the draw process. Unlike traditional loans where funds are disbursed in a lump sum, construction loans release funds in stages based on project milestones. This process ensures that funds are used appropriately and that the project is progressing as planned. Borrowers submit draw requests, which are reviewed and approved by the lender before funds are released. Understanding how to manage this process is crucial to maintaining cash flow and avoiding delays. Effective coordination with your contractor and lender ensures that each phase of construction is completed smoothly.

Risk management is also a central theme in SBA construction financing. Construction projects involve multiple variables, including cost fluctuations, labor availability, and regulatory requirements. Successful borrowers anticipate these risks and develop strategies to mitigate them. This includes selecting experienced contractors, conducting thorough due diligence, and maintaining clear communication throughout the project. By proactively addressing potential challenges, you can minimize disruptions and increase the likelihood of a successful outcome.

As you progress through this book, you will gain a deeper understanding of how to structure SBA construction loans, navigate the approval process, and execute projects with confidence. This chapter serves as your foundation, providing the knowledge you need to approach construction financing strategically. By mastering these principles, you will be positioned to leverage SBA programs effectively and transform your vision into reality. Construction is not just about building structures—it is about building opportunities, creating value, and establishing a legacy of growth and success.

Real-Life Math Example: SBA Construction Loan for a Medical Office Expansion

Imagine a business owner named David who operates a successful medical clinic that has outgrown its current space. Demand for his services has increased significantly, and he needs a larger facility to accommodate more patients, staff, and equipment. Instead of leasing additional space, David decides to build a new 6,000-square-foot medical office building using SBA construction financing. His goal is not only to expand his operations but also to own the real estate, build equity, and create long-term financial stability. David identifies a piece of land priced at $400,000. After working with an architect and contractor, he determines that the cost to construct the building will be $1,200,000. In addition to construction costs, he estimates $150,000 for soft costs, including architectural fees, permits, engineering, and inspections. He also sets aside a 10% contingency reserve of $120,000 to account for unexpected expenses. This brings the total project cost to $1,870,000.

Using an SBA loan structure, David is required to put down 10% of the total project cost. This means his equity injection is $187,000. The remaining $1,683,000 is financed through the SBA loan. This lower down payment allows David to preserve capital for other business needs, such as purchasing new medical equipment and hiring additional staff.

The loan is structured with a 25-year amortization and an interest rate of 7%. David's monthly payment can be calculated using standard loan amortization formulas. With a loan amount of $1,683,000 at 7% over 25 years, his monthly principal and interest payment is approximately $11,900. This payment replaces the rent he was previously paying, which was $9,500 per month. While his payment is higher, he is now building equity and owning a valuable asset.

Once construction is complete, the new building is appraised at $2,300,000 due to its modern design, larger size, and improved functionality. This creates immediate equity of $430,000 ($2,300,000 value minus $1,870,000 total cost). This increase in value demonstrates the power of construction financing as a wealth-building tool.

David's expanded facility allows him to increase patient capacity by 50%. As a result, his monthly revenue increases from $80,000 to $120,000. After accounting for additional expenses, his net income increases by $20,000 per month. This additional income more than offsets the higher loan payment, resulting in improved cash flow and profitability.

In addition to his primary operations, David leases out 1,500 square feet of unused space to another medical professional for $3,000 per month. This rental income further enhances his financial position, effectively reducing his net occupancy cost. When combined with his increased business revenue, the expansion significantly improves his overall financial performance.

Over time, as David pays down his loan and property values continue to rise, his equity grows even further. After 10 years, he has paid down a substantial portion of the loan, and the property has appreciated to $2,800,000. His remaining loan balance is approximately $1,300,000, giving him $1,500,000 in equity. This equity can be leveraged for future investments, additional expansions, or other business opportunities. This example illustrates how SBA construction financing can transform a business. By leveraging a relatively small down payment, David was able to build a high-value asset, increase his revenue, and create long-term wealth. The key to his success was understanding the numbers, structuring the deal correctly, and executing his project with precision. When used strategically, SBA construction loans are not just a financing tool—they are a catalyst for growth, expansion, and financial independence.

Chapter 2

Structuring SBA Construction and Expansion Mortgage Loans for Maximum Approval and Efficiency

Structuring an SBA construction and expansion mortgage loan correctly is one of the most critical steps in ensuring both approval and long-term success. While many borrowers focus primarily on qualifying for the loan, experienced investors and business owners understand that how a deal is structured can significantly impact cash flow, risk, scalability, and future opportunities. SBA-backed financing through the U.S. Small Business Administration provides flexibility, but that flexibility must be used strategically. A well-structured deal aligns the borrower's financial strength, the project's feasibility, and the lender's requirements into a cohesive plan that minimizes risk while maximizing return.

At the core of structuring an SBA construction loan is understanding the full scope of the project. This includes not only the cost of land and construction but also soft costs, reserves, working capital, and operational needs. Many borrowers underestimate the importance of including all relevant expenses in the loan structure, which can lead to funding gaps during construction. A properly structured loan anticipates every phase of the project—from acquisition to completion to stabilization—ensuring that sufficient capital is available at each stage. This level of planning demonstrates to lenders that the borrower is prepared and capable of managing a complex development.

One of the most important decisions in structuring an SBA construction loan is choosing between SBA 7(a) and SBA 504 financing. Each program has distinct advantages, and selecting the right one depends on the borrower's goals. The SBA 7(a) program offers greater flexibility, allowing borrowers to finance construction, equipment, working capital, and even business acquisition costs within a single loan. This makes it ideal for projects that require a comprehensive financing solution. On the other hand, the SBA 504 program is designed for long-term, fixed-rate financing of owner-occupied real estate and is often used for larger construction projects. It typically involves a partnership between a bank and a Certified Development Company (CDC), resulting in lower fixed interest rates and structured financing that includes multiple components.

Another critical aspect of loan structuring is the loan-to-cost (LTC) ratio. SBA construction loans often allow financing up to 90% of the total project cost, meaning the borrower contributes approximately 10% as equity. However, this percentage can vary depending on factors such as the borrower's experience, credit profile, and the complexity of the project. Structuring your equity injection strategically is essential. This can include cash, land equity, or even value created through project planning. For example, if you already own the land, its appraised value may count toward your equity requirement, reducing the amount of cash needed at closing.

Debt service coverage ratio (DSCR) is another key component in structuring SBA construction loans. Lenders use DSCR to evaluate whether the projected income from the property or business will be sufficient to cover the loan payments. A DSCR of 1.25 or higher is typically required, meaning the property or business generates at least 25% more income than the debt obligations. Structuring your deal to meet or exceed this threshold is critical for approval. This may involve adjusting project scope, increasing projected revenue, or reducing costs to improve financial performance.

Interest rates and amortization terms also play a significant role in structuring the loan. SBA loans typically offer longer amortization periods—up to 25 years for real estate—which results in lower monthly payments compared to shorter-term loans. During the construction phase, many SBA loans allow for interest-only payments, reducing the financial burden while the project is being built. Once construction is complete, the loan transitions into a fully amortizing structure. Understanding how these phases work and how they impact your cash flow is essential for maintaining financial stability throughout the project.

Another important consideration is the inclusion of working capital within the loan structure. Construction projects often require additional funds beyond the physical build, including hiring staff, purchasing equipment, and covering operating expenses during the ramp-up period. SBA 7(a) loans, in particular, allow borrowers to include working capital as part of the financing package. This ensures that the business can operate effectively once the project is completed, reducing the risk of cash flow shortages during the transition.

Collateral and guarantees are also integral to SBA loan structuring. While the primary collateral is typically the property being constructed or renovated, lenders may require additional collateral depending on the loan size and risk profile. Personal guarantees are standard for SBA loans, meaning the borrower is personally responsible for repayment. Structuring your assets and understanding your risk exposure is an important part of the process. Experienced borrowers often work with financial advisors to ensure that their overall financial position is protected while still meeting lender requirements. Timing is another critical factor in structuring SBA construction loans. From application to approval to funding, the process can take several months. Coordinating this timeline with your construction schedule is essential to avoid delays. This includes securing permits, finalizing construction plans, and selecting contractors before closing. A well-structured timeline ensures that the project can begin immediately after funding, minimizing holding costs and accelerating completion.

Another advanced strategy in structuring SBA construction loans is phasing the project. Instead of building everything at once, some borrowers choose to complete construction in stages. This approach can reduce initial costs, improve cash flow, and allow the project to generate income sooner. For example, a business owner might build a portion of a facility first, begin operations, and then expand further once revenue increases. This phased approach can make larger projects more manageable and reduce overall risk.

Ultimately, structuring an SBA construction and expansion mortgage loan is about aligning all components of the deal—financial, operational, and strategic—into a cohesive plan. It requires careful analysis, detailed planning, and a clear understanding of both lender requirements and business goals. When done correctly, the structure of your loan becomes a powerful tool that supports your growth, enhances your cash flow, and positions you for long-term success. This chapter provides the framework for making informed decisions, ensuring that your project is not only approved but also optimized for maximum performance.

Real-Life Math Example: Structuring an SBA Construction Loan for a Multi-Tenant Office Expansion

Consider a business owner named Maria who owns a successful consulting firm and wants to expand into a larger, multi-tenant office building. Her goal is to occupy part of the building for her business while leasing the remaining space to generate additional income. This strategy allows her to meet SBA owner-occupancy requirements while creating a secondary revenue stream.

Maria identifies a property where she can construct a 10,000-square-foot building. The land costs $500,000, and construction is estimated at $2,000,000. Soft costs, including architectural design, permits, and engineering, total $200,000. She also includes a contingency reserve of $200,000. This brings the total project cost to $2,900,000.

Maria chooses an SBA 504 loan structure. In this structure, she contributes 10% equity, or $290,000. The bank finances

50% of the project, or $1,450,000, while the CDC finances 40%, or $1,160,000. The bank portion carries a variable interest rate of 6.5%, while the CDC portion has a fixed rate of 5.5%. Both loans are amortized over 25 years.

Maria's monthly payment for the bank portion is approximately $9,800, while the CDC portion is about $7,100, resulting in a total monthly payment of $16,900. To evaluate feasibility, Maria calculates the projected income from the building. Her consulting business will occupy 5,500 square feet, while the remaining 4,500 square feet will be leased at $25 per square foot annually.

This results in annual rental income of $112,500, or $9,375 per month. Additionally, Maria estimates that her business will generate $30,000 more per month due to increased capacity and improved operations. Combining rental income and business growth, her total monthly income increase is approximately $39,375.

After subtracting the loan payment of $16,900, Maria has a net positive cash flow of $22,475 per month. This demonstrates a strong DSCR, well above the lender's requirement. The project not only meets approval criteria but also significantly enhances Maria's financial position.

Upon completion, the property is appraised at $3,500,000, creating immediate equity of $600,000. Over time, as rents increase and the property appreciates, this equity continues to grow. After 10 years, assuming a conservative appreciation rate, the property value reaches $4,200,000, while the loan balance decreases to approximately $2,200,000. Maria now has $2,000,000 in equity.

This structured approach allows Maria to achieve multiple objectives simultaneously: expanding her business, generating passive income, and building long-term wealth. By carefully structuring her SBA construction loan, she minimizes risk, maximizes cash flow, and creates a scalable investment that supports future growth.

Chapter 3

The SBA Construction Loan Approval Process Step-by-Step

Securing approval for an SBA construction and expansion mortgage loan is one of the most important stages in turning your vision into reality. While many borrowers focus on the idea of building or expanding, the approval process is where projects are either validated or denied. Understanding how this process works—from the lender's perspective—is critical to positioning your deal for success. SBA-backed financing through the U.S. Small Business Administration follows a structured, detailed, and highly documented process designed to minimize risk while supporting viable business growth. Borrowers who understand this process and prepare accordingly dramatically increase their chances of approval and smooth execution.

The first step in the SBA construction loan approval process is prequalification. This is where the lender evaluates your basic financial profile to determine whether you are a viable candidate. Key factors include your personal credit score, business financials, experience, liquidity, and overall debt obligations. Lenders are not just looking for strong numbers—they are looking for a borrower who demonstrates financial discipline and the ability to manage a complex project. During this phase, it is essential to present organized documentation, including tax returns, financial statements, and a clear summary of your project. A strong prequalification sets the tone for the entire approval process.

Once prequalified, the next step is project evaluation. Unlike traditional loans, construction financing requires lenders to analyze the feasibility of the project itself. This includes reviewing construction plans, budgets, timelines, and the overall purpose of the development. Lenders want to ensure that the project makes sense both financially and operationally. For example, if you are building a retail space, they will evaluate market demand, location, and potential revenue. If you are expanding a business, they will assess whether the expansion aligns with your growth strategy. This step is critical because even a financially strong borrower can be denied if the project itself is not viable.

The third step is assembling the full loan package. This is one of the most detailed parts of the process and requires careful attention to detail. The loan package typically includes personal and business tax returns, financial statements, a business plan, construction plans, contractor agreements, and a detailed project budget. Additionally, lenders often require a pro forma, which is a financial projection showing how the project will perform once completed. This projection must demonstrate that the project will generate enough income to cover the loan payments while maintaining a healthy debt service coverage ratio. A well-prepared loan package not only improves your chances of approval but also speeds up the underwriting process.

Underwriting is the next stage, and it is where the lender conducts a deep analysis of both the borrower and the project. This includes verifying all financial information, analyzing cash flow, and assessing risk. Underwriters will scrutinize every aspect of the deal, including credit history, income stability, project feasibility, and collateral value. They will also evaluate the experience of the borrower and the construction team. For first-time developers, this can be a challenge, as lenders prefer borrowers with proven experience. However, this can be mitigated by partnering with experienced contractors and consultants who bring credibility to the project.

A critical component of underwriting is the appraisal and feasibility analysis. The lender will order an appraisal to determine the projected value of the property once construction is complete. This is known as the "as-completed" value. The appraisal must support the loan amount and demonstrate that the project will create sufficient value. In addition to the appraisal, lenders may conduct a feasibility study to assess market conditions, demand, and potential risks. These analyses provide an objective evaluation of the project and are essential for final approval.

After underwriting, the loan moves into the approval and commitment stage. If the lender is satisfied with the analysis, they will issue a loan commitment outlining the terms and conditions of the loan. This includes the loan amount, interest rate, repayment terms, and any conditions that must be met before closing. It is important to review this commitment carefully and ensure that all terms align with your expectations. This stage may also involve negotiations to finalize certain aspects of the deal.

The closing process is the final step before construction begins. During closing, all legal documents are signed, and the loan is officially funded. This includes finalizing construction contracts, securing permits, and ensuring that all conditions have been met. Once the loan is closed, funds are not typically disbursed all at once. Instead, they are released through a draw process as construction progresses. Understanding this process is essential for managing your project effectively.

One of the most important aspects of the approval process is communication. Maintaining clear and consistent communication with your lender, contractor, and other stakeholders ensures that the process moves smoothly. Delays often occur due to missing documentation, unclear information, or lack of coordination. By staying organized and proactive, you can avoid these issues and keep your project on track.

Another key factor in approval is demonstrating experience and credibility. Lenders want to see that you have the ability to execute the project successfully. This does not necessarily mean you need to have completed similar projects in the past, but you must show that you have a capable team in place. This includes hiring experienced contractors, working with knowledgeable advisors, and presenting a clear and realistic plan. Credibility is built through preparation, professionalism, and attention to detail.

Risk mitigation is also a central focus of the approval process. Lenders will look for potential risks and evaluate how they are addressed. This includes construction risks, market risks, and financial risks. Providing contingency plans, realistic budgets, and conservative projections demonstrates that you have considered these risks and are prepared to manage them. This level of preparation not only improves your chances of approval but also sets the foundation for a successful project.

Ultimately, the SBA construction loan approval process is about proving that your project is viable, your finances are strong, and your execution plan is sound. While the process may seem complex, it is designed to ensure that only well-prepared and feasible projects move forward. By understanding each step and preparing thoroughly, you can navigate the process with confidence and position yourself for success. Approval is not just about meeting requirements—it is about presenting a compelling case that your project is worth funding and capable of delivering long-term value.

Real-Life Math Example: SBA Construction Loan Approval for a Retail Expansion Project

Consider a business owner named James who owns a growing retail store and wants to expand into a larger, newly constructed commercial space. His current store generates $70,000 per month in revenue, but he has reached capacity and cannot serve additional customers. After analyzing market demand, he decides to build a new 8,000-square-foot retail building to increase his sales and improve customer experience.

James identifies a project with the following costs: land acquisition at $300,000, construction costs of $1,500,000, soft costs of $150,000, and a contingency reserve of $150,000. This brings the total project cost to $2,100,000. To move forward with SBA financing, James must contribute a 10% down payment, which equals $210,000. The remaining $1,890,000 is financed through an SBA loan. During prequalification, James presents his financials, showing consistent revenue growth and a strong credit profile. His personal credit score is 720, and his business financials demonstrate stable cash flow. This initial evaluation positions him as a strong candidate for financing. However, the lender must also evaluate whether the expanded store will generate enough income to support the new loan.

The loan is structured with a 25-year amortization at an interest rate of 7%. Based on these terms, James's monthly payment is approximately $13,400. To determine whether the project meets the lender's requirements, a debt service coverage ratio analysis is performed. The lender requires a DSCR of at least 1.25, meaning James must generate at least $16,750 per month in net income to support the loan.

James works with his accountant to create a pro forma projection. Based on increased space and improved layout, he estimates that his monthly revenue will grow from $70,000 to $110,000. After accounting for additional operating expenses, his projected net income is $25,000 per month. This results in a DSCR of approximately 1.87 ($25,000 divided by $13,400), which exceeds the lender's requirement and strengthens his application.

The lender then orders an appraisal, which estimates the completed property value at $2,600,000. This supports the loan amount and demonstrates that the project will create additional equity. The difference between the appraised value and total project cost is $500,000, representing immediate value creation upon completion.

During underwriting, the lender reviews James's financials, project plans, and contractor agreements. They confirm that the construction timeline is realistic and that the budget includes sufficient contingency reserves. They also evaluate the local market and determine that demand for retail space in the area is strong. This comprehensive analysis reduces perceived risk and supports approval.

Once approved, James receives a loan commitment outlining the terms and conditions. He proceeds to closing, where all documents are finalized, and construction begins. Funds are disbursed in stages through the draw process, ensuring that each phase of construction is completed before additional funds are released.

After completion, James's new store opens and quickly achieves the projected revenue increase. His monthly net income rises to $25,000, and he comfortably covers his loan payments. Over time, as his business continues to grow and property values increase, his equity position strengthens. Five years later, the property is valued at $3,200,000, and James has paid down his loan balance to $1,700,000. This gives him $1,500,000 in equity. Additionally, his business revenue has grown to $140,000 per month, further improving his financial position.

This example demonstrates how understanding and navigating the SBA construction loan approval process can lead to significant financial growth. By preparing thoroughly, structuring the deal correctly, and presenting a strong case to the lender, James was able to secure financing, expand his business, and build long-term wealth.

Chapter 4

Managing the SBA Construction Process and Draw Schedule Successfully

Once your SBA construction and expansion mortgage loan has been approved and closed, the real work begins. Many borrowers believe that securing financing is the hardest part of the process, but in reality, execution is where projects are won or lost. Managing construction effectively requires discipline, organization, and a deep understanding of how funds are disbursed, how timelines are maintained, and how risks are controlled. SBA-backed construction financing through the U.S. Small Business Administration is designed to support structured, well-managed projects, and understanding the mechanics of this system is essential to ensuring your success.

The construction phase is fundamentally different from the approval phase because it involves real-time decision-making, coordination between multiple parties, and strict adherence to budgets and timelines. At the center of this phase is the draw schedule, which is the process by which loan funds are released in stages as construction progresses. Unlike traditional loans that provide a lump sum, SBA construction loans are disbursed incrementally to ensure that funds are used appropriately and that the project is advancing according to plan. This system protects both the lender and the borrower, but it also requires careful management to avoid delays and disruptions.

The draw process typically begins after an initial equity injection from the borrower. This means that before loan funds are disbursed, you are required to invest your portion of the project cost. This ensures that you have a vested interest in the project and reduces the lender's risk. Once your equity has been deployed, the lender begins releasing funds based on completed work. Each draw corresponds to a specific phase of construction, such as site preparation, foundation, framing, electrical and plumbing, and final finishes. Understanding these phases and aligning your budget accordingly is critical to maintaining cash flow.

One of the most important aspects of managing the draw schedule is documentation. Each time you request funds, you must provide evidence that the work has been completed. This typically includes invoices, receipts, contractor statements, and inspection reports. The lender may also require a third-party inspection to verify progress before approving the draw. This process ensures that funds are being used correctly, but it can also create delays if documentation is incomplete or inaccurate. Staying organized and maintaining clear records is essential to keeping the process moving smoothly.

Communication is another critical component of successful construction management. You must maintain constant communication with your contractor, lender, and any other stakeholders involved in the project. Miscommunication can lead to delays, cost overruns, and even disputes. For example, if a contractor completes work but does not submit the required documentation promptly, the draw may be delayed, impacting the entire project timeline. By establishing clear communication protocols and expectations from the beginning, you can avoid these issues and ensure that everyone is aligned.

Budget management is equally important during the construction phase. Even with a well-structured loan, unexpected costs can arise. Material prices may increase, labor shortages may occur, or unforeseen site conditions may require additional work. This is why contingency reserves are included in SBA construction loans. Typically set at 5% to 10% of the total project cost, these reserves provide a financial buffer to handle unexpected expenses. However, using these funds wisely is critical. Poor budget management can deplete your reserves quickly, leaving you vulnerable to financial strain.

Another key factor in managing construction is timeline control. Delays are one of the most common challenges in construction projects, and they can have a significant impact on your financial performance. Extended timelines increase carrying costs, including interest payments, insurance, and taxes, while also delaying the generation of revenue. To mitigate this risk, it is essential to work with experienced contractors who have a proven track record of completing projects on time. Additionally, setting realistic timelines and building in buffers for potential delays can help you stay on track.

Inspections play a crucial role in the draw process and overall project management. Lenders often require inspections at various stages of construction to ensure that work is completed according to plan. These inspections provide an additional layer of oversight and help identify potential issues early. While inspections can sometimes feel like an added hurdle, they ultimately protect your investment by ensuring quality and compliance. Being prepared for inspections and addressing any issues promptly is key to maintaining progress.

Another advanced strategy in managing SBA construction projects is sequencing work efficiently. The order in which tasks are completed can significantly impact both timelines and costs. For example, delays in foundation work can push back the entire project, while efficient coordination between trades can accelerate completion. Working closely with your contractor to develop a detailed construction schedule ensures that each phase is executed in the correct order and that resources are used effectively. Cash flow management during construction is also critical. Even though the loan provides funding, there may be periods where expenses are incurred before draw funds are received. This requires careful planning to ensure that you have sufficient liquidity to cover short-term costs. Some borrowers maintain a separate reserve fund to manage these gaps, while others negotiate favorable payment terms with contractors. Understanding your cash flow cycle and planning accordingly prevents disruptions and keeps your project moving forward.

Risk management during construction extends beyond financial considerations. Safety, compliance, and regulatory requirements must all be addressed. This includes obtaining necessary permits, adhering to building codes, and ensuring that all work is performed safely. Failure to comply with these requirements can result in fines, delays, or even project shutdowns. Working with qualified professionals and staying informed about local regulations ensures that your project remains compliant.

As construction nears completion, the focus shifts to final inspections, occupancy permits, and transitioning into the operational phase. This is where your project begins to generate revenue and deliver the returns you envisioned. Properly managing the final stages of construction ensures a smooth transition and sets the stage for long-term success. This includes completing all punch list items, finalizing documentation, and ensuring that the property is ready for use or occupancy.

Ultimately, managing the SBA construction process and draw schedule is about execution. It requires attention to detail, proactive planning, and effective communication. While challenges are inevitable, a well-managed project can overcome these obstacles and achieve outstanding results. By understanding how the draw process works, maintaining control over your budget and timeline, and staying organized throughout the project, you can successfully navigate the construction phase and bring your vision to life.

Real-Life Math Example: Managing the Draw Schedule for a Warehouse Construction Project

Consider a business owner named Alex who is constructing a 12,000-square-foot warehouse to expand his logistics company. The total project cost is $3,000,000, which includes $600,000 for land, $2,000,000 for construction, $200,000 for soft costs, and a $200,000 contingency reserve. Alex contributes a 10% down payment of $300,000, and the remaining $2,700,000 is financed through an SBA construction loan.

The construction is divided into five major phases: site preparation, foundation, structural framing, systems installation (electrical, plumbing, HVAC), and final finishes. Each phase corresponds to a portion of the total construction budget. Site preparation is allocated $300,000, foundation $400,000, framing $700,000, systems $400,000, and finishes $200,000. The remaining $200,000 is reserved for contingencies.

At the start of the project, Alex injects his $300,000 equity, which is used to cover initial costs, including land preparation and early construction expenses. Once this equity is fully utilized, the lender begins disbursing funds through the draw process. After completing site preparation, Alex submits a draw request for $300,000. The lender reviews the documentation, conducts an inspection, and approves the draw, releasing funds to reimburse the completed work.

As the project progresses, each phase follows a similar process. After completing the foundation, Alex submits a draw request for $400,000. The lender verifies the work and releases the funds. This continues through each phase, with draw requests for $700,000 for framing, $400,000 for systems, and

$200,000 for finishes. In total, the lender disburses $2,000,000 for construction costs, along with additional funds for soft costs and contingencies as needed.

During construction, Alex encounters an unexpected increase in material costs, adding $100,000 to the budget. He uses part of the contingency reserve to cover this expense, ensuring that the project continues without disruption. This highlights the importance of including contingency funds in the loan structure.

The construction timeline is 12 months. During this period, Alex makes interest-only payments on the loan. Assuming an interest rate of 7% on the $2,700,000 loan, his monthly interest payment is approximately $15,750. Over 12 months, this totals $189,000 in interest payments. While this is a significant cost, it is necessary to complete the project and achieve long-term gains.

Upon completion, the warehouse is operational and increases Alex's business capacity by 60%. His monthly revenue grows from $150,000 to $240,000, while his net income increases by $35,000 per month. The loan transitions into a fully amortizing structure, with a monthly payment of approximately $19,000.

After accounting for the new loan payment, Alex still achieves a net increase in cash flow of $16,000 per month. Additionally, the property is appraised at $3,800,000, creating immediate equity of $800,000. Over time, as the loan balance decreases and the property appreciates, Alex's equity continues to grow.

Five years later, the property value reaches $4,500,000, and the loan balance is reduced to $2,300,000. This results in $2,200,000 in equity. Combined with the increased profitability of his business, Alex's financial position is significantly stronger than before the project.

This example demonstrates the importance of managing the draw schedule effectively. By understanding how funds are disbursed, maintaining control over the budget, and addressing challenges proactively, Alex was able to complete his project successfully and achieve substantial financial growth.

Chapter 5

Choosing the Right SBA Loan Program for Construction and Expansion Projects

Selecting the right financing structure is one of the most important decisions you will make when planning a construction or expansion project. While SBA-backed financing offers powerful advantages, not all SBA loan programs are the same. Understanding how to choose between them—and how to align each option with your specific goals—is critical to achieving both approval and long-term success. Programs supported by the U.S. Small Business Administration are designed to provide flexibility and support growth, but the effectiveness of these programs depends on how well they are matched to your project.

The two primary SBA loan programs used for construction and expansion are the SBA 7(a) and SBA 504 loans. Each program serves a different purpose, and choosing the right one depends on the nature of your project, your financial profile, and your long-term objectives. The SBA 7(a) program is known for its flexibility. It allows borrowers to finance a wide range of expenses, including land acquisition, construction, equipment, working capital, and even business acquisition. This makes it an ideal choice for projects that require a comprehensive financing solution, especially when the borrower needs additional funds beyond the physical construction.

In contrast, the SBA 504 loan program is specifically designed for long-term, fixed-rate financing of owner-occupied commercial real estate. It is often used for larger construction projects where stability and predictable payments are priorities. The 504 program typically involves two lenders: a bank that finances approximately 50% of the project and a Certified Development Company (CDC) that finances around 40%, with the borrower contributing 10% as equity. This structure allows borrowers to benefit from lower fixed interest rates on the CDC portion while maintaining manageable down payment requirements.

One of the key differences between the 7(a) and 504 programs is how funds can be used. The 7(a) loan offers greater flexibility, allowing you to include working capital, inventory, and other business-related expenses. This is particularly useful for businesses that need additional support during the transition into a new or expanded facility. The 504 loan, on the other hand, is more focused on fixed assets such as land, buildings, and long-term equipment. It does not typically cover working capital, which means borrowers may need to secure additional financing if they require operational funds.

Interest rates and repayment structures also differ between the two programs. SBA 7(a) loans often have variable interest rates tied to market conditions, while SBA 504 loans offer fixed rates on the CDC portion, providing greater predictability over time. For borrowers who prioritize stability and long-term planning, the fixed-rate component of the 504 loan can be a significant advantage. However, those who value flexibility and the ability to adjust their financing may prefer the 7(a) program.

Another important consideration is the size and scope of the project. Larger construction projects often align well with the SBA 504 program due to its structured financing and lower fixed rates. Smaller or more complex projects that involve multiple components—such as construction combined with business acquisition or operational expansion—may be better suited for the 7(a) program. Understanding the scale of your project and how it aligns with each program is essential to making the right choice.

Owner-occupancy requirements also play a role in determining which program is appropriate. Both SBA 7(a) and 504 loans require the borrower to occupy a significant portion of the property, typically at least 51% for existing buildings and

60% for new construction. This requirement ensures that the financing supports active businesses rather than purely passive investments. However, both programs still allow for leasing a portion of the property, creating an additional income stream.

Another key factor in choosing the right program is your long-term strategy. If your goal is to build a property and hold it for many years, benefiting from stable payments and long-term appreciation, the SBA 504 program may be the better choice. If your strategy involves flexibility, potential refinancing, or combining multiple business needs into a single loan, the SBA 7(a) program may be more suitable. Aligning your financing with your long-term goals ensures that your loan structure supports your overall strategy.

Down payment requirements are also an important consideration. Both programs typically require a minimum of 10% equity, but this can increase depending on factors such as the borrower's experience, the type of property, and the level of risk. For example, startup businesses or special-purpose properties may require higher equity contributions. Understanding these requirements and planning accordingly is essential to ensuring that you have sufficient capital to move forward.

Another advanced consideration is the potential to combine financing strategies. In some cases, borrowers may use an SBA 504 loan for the real estate portion of the project while securing separate financing for working capital or other needs. This hybrid approach allows you to take advantage of the strengths of each financing option while addressing the full scope of your project.

The approval process for each program also differs slightly. SBA 7(a) loans are often processed more quickly due to their flexibility, while SBA 504 loans may involve additional steps due to the involvement of the CDC. Understanding the timeline and requirements for each program allows you to plan your project more effectively and avoid delays.

Another important aspect of choosing the right program is working with experienced lenders. Not all lenders have the same level of expertise in SBA construction financing, and selecting a lender who understands your project and the nuances of each program can make a significant difference. Experienced lenders can guide you through the decision-making process, help structure your deal, and ensure that your application is presented effectively.

Ultimately, choosing the right SBA loan program is about aligning your financing with your project, your business, and your long-term goals. It requires a clear understanding of the options available and a strategic approach to decision-making. By selecting the program that best fits your needs, you set the foundation for a successful project and position yourself for long-term growth.

Real-Life Math Example: Choosing Between SBA 7(a) and SBA 504 for a Construction Project

Consider a business owner named Steven who plans to build a new 7,500-square-foot office building. The total project cost is $2,500,000, including $500,000 for land, $1,700,000 for construction, and $300,000 for soft costs and contingencies. Steven must decide whether to use an SBA 7(a) loan or an SBA 504 loan to finance the project.

If Steven chooses the SBA 7(a) loan, he can finance the entire project, including an additional $200,000 in working capital to support his business during the transition. This brings the total loan amount to $2,700,000. With a 10% down payment, Steven contributes $270,000, and the loan amount is $2,430,000. At a 7% interest rate over 25 years, his monthly payment is approximately $17,200.

The advantage of this structure is flexibility. Steven has access to working capital, which helps him cover operating expenses, hire staff, and manage cash flow during the early stages of the project. His business generates an additional $30,000 per month in net income after expansion, allowing him to comfortably cover the loan payment and achieve positive cash flow.

Alternatively, Steven considers the SBA 504 loan. In this structure, he contributes 10% equity, or $250,000. The bank finances 50% of the project, or $1,250,000, while the CDC finances 40%, or $1,000,000. The bank portion has a variable interest rate of 6.5%, while the CDC portion has a fixed rate of 5.5%.

Steven's monthly payment for the bank portion is approximately $8,400, while the CDC portion is about $6,100, resulting in a total monthly payment of $14,500. This lower payment improves his cash flow compared to the 7(a) option. However, he does not have access to the additional $200,000 in working capital, which means he must rely on his own reserves or secure separate financing.

After analyzing both options, Steven determines that the SBA 7(a) loan is better suited to his needs because of the additional working capital. Although the monthly payment is higher, the flexibility and financial support during the transition period provide greater overall stability. If his primary goal had been to minimize monthly payments and focus solely on real estate, the SBA 504 loan would have been the better choice. This example illustrates how the choice between SBA 7(a) and SBA 504 loans depends on the specific needs of the borrower. By understanding the differences and analyzing the financial impact of each option, Steven is able to select the program that aligns with his goals and supports the success of his project.

Chapter 6

Risk Management and Cost Control in SBA Construction and Expansion Projects

Risk is an unavoidable part of any construction and expansion project, but the difference between successful and failed developments often comes down to how well that risk is managed. When using SBA-backed financing through the U.S. Small Business Administration, lenders place a strong emphasis on risk mitigation because construction projects involve multiple moving parts, large capital investments, and potential uncertainties. For borrowers, understanding how to identify, manage, and control risk is essential not only for getting approved but for completing the project on time, within budget, and with strong financial outcomes. This chapter focuses on building a disciplined approach to risk management and cost control that protects your investment and maximizes your return.

The first step in effective risk management is identifying the different types of risks involved in construction projects. These typically fall into several categories: financial risk, construction risk, market risk, operational risk, and regulatory risk. Financial risk includes interest rate fluctuations, cost overruns, and cash flow shortages. Construction risk involves delays, contractor performance issues, and material cost increases. Market risk relates to changes in demand, competition, and economic conditions. Operational risk includes challenges in running the business after completion, while regulatory risk involves compliance with zoning, permits, and building codes. By recognizing these categories early, you can develop strategies to address each one proactively.

One of the most critical tools for managing financial risk is the project budget. A detailed and realistic budget is the foundation of any successful construction project. This includes not only hard costs such as labor and materials but also soft costs like architectural fees, permits, legal expenses, and inspections. Additionally, contingency reserves must be included to account for unexpected expenses. SBA lenders typically require a contingency of 5% to 10% of the total project cost, but experienced borrowers often plan conservatively and allocate sufficient reserves to handle worst-case scenarios. A well-prepared budget demonstrates to lenders that you understand the full scope of the project and are prepared for potential challenges.

Cost control is closely tied to budgeting, but it extends into the execution phase of the project. Once construction begins, it is essential to monitor expenses closely and compare them against the budget. This requires regular tracking of invoices, draw requests, and overall spending. Small deviations can quickly escalate into significant cost overruns if not addressed promptly. Establishing a system for tracking costs and reviewing financial performance on a regular basis allows you to identify issues early and take corrective action before they become major problems.

Another important aspect of cost control is contractor selection. The quality and reliability of your contractor have a direct impact on both the timeline and the budget of your project. Choosing the lowest bid may seem attractive initially, but it can lead to higher costs in the long run if the contractor lacks experience or fails to deliver quality work. Experienced contractors may charge more upfront, but they often complete projects more efficiently and with fewer issues. Conducting thorough due diligence, checking references, and reviewing past projects are essential steps in selecting the right contractor.

Fixed-price contracts are another effective tool for managing construction risk. By agreeing on a fixed price for the project, you can limit your exposure to cost increases. However, it is important to ensure that the contract is detailed and clearly defines the scope of work, materials, and timelines. Ambiguities in the contract can lead to disputes and additional costs. In some cases, hybrid contracts that combine fixed and variable components may be appropriate, depending on the nature of the project.

Material cost volatility is another significant risk in construction projects. Prices for materials such as steel, lumber, and concrete can fluctuate due to market conditions, supply chain disruptions, and economic factors. To mitigate this risk, some borrowers lock in prices early through contracts or bulk purchasing agreements. Others include escalation clauses in their contracts to account for potential increases. Understanding how material costs impact your budget and planning accordingly is essential for maintaining financial stability.

Time is another critical factor in risk management. Delays can significantly increase costs by extending the construction timeline and increasing carrying expenses such as interest, insurance, and taxes. Effective project scheduling and timeline management are essential to minimizing delays. This includes setting realistic deadlines, coordinating with contractors and suppliers, and anticipating potential obstacles. Building buffer time into your schedule can help absorb unexpected delays without disrupting the overall project. Cash flow management is also a key component of risk control. Even with SBA financing, there may be periods where expenses exceed available funds due to the timing of draw disbursements. Maintaining a cash reserve or line of credit can help bridge these gaps and ensure that the project continues without interruption. Understanding the timing of your expenses and draw schedule allows you to plan effectively and avoid cash flow shortages.

Insurance is another important tool for managing risk. Construction projects require various types of insurance coverage, including builder's risk insurance, general liability insurance, and workers' compensation. These policies protect against potential losses resulting from accidents, damage, or other unforeseen events. Ensuring that you have adequate insurance coverage in place is essential for protecting your investment and minimizing financial exposure.

Regulatory compliance is often overlooked but can have significant consequences if not managed properly. Construction projects must comply with local zoning laws, building codes, and permit requirements. Failure to meet these requirements can result in fines, delays, or even project shutdowns. Working with experienced professionals and staying informed about regulatory requirements ensures that your project remains compliant and avoids unnecessary complications. Another advanced strategy in risk management is scenario planning. This involves analyzing different potential outcomes and preparing strategies for each scenario. For example, what happens if construction costs increase by 10%? What if the project is delayed by three months? What if market conditions change? By considering these scenarios in advance, you can develop contingency plans and make informed decisions during the project.

Ultimately, risk management and cost control are about maintaining control over your project. While you cannot eliminate all risks, you can minimize their impact through careful planning, disciplined execution, and proactive decision-making. SBA construction financing provides the framework and resources to support your project, but it is your responsibility to manage the process effectively. By mastering these principles, you can protect your investment, ensure successful completion, and achieve your long-term financial goals.

Real-Life Math Example: Managing Risk and Cost Control in a Restaurant Construction Project

Consider a business owner named Lisa who is building a new restaurant using SBA construction financing. The total project cost is $2,500,000, which includes $500,000 for land,

$1,600,000 for construction, $200,000 for soft costs, and a $200,000 contingency reserve. Lisa contributes a 10% down payment of $250,000, and the remaining $2,250,000 is financed through an SBA loan.

Lisa creates a detailed budget that breaks down construction costs into specific categories. These include $600,000 for structural work, $400,000 for interior build-out, $300,000 for kitchen equipment, $200,000 for electrical and plumbing, and $100,000 for finishes. This level of detail allows her to track expenses closely and identify any deviations from the budget.

During construction, Lisa encounters a 15% increase in material costs for steel and lumber, adding $120,000 to her project. Because she included a $200,000 contingency reserve, she is able to cover this increase without disrupting the project. After using $120,000, she still has $80,000 remaining in her contingency fund.

Lisa also experiences a two-month delay due to supply chain issues. This delay increases her carrying costs, including interest payments. With an interest rate of 7% on her $2,250,000 loan, her monthly interest payment during construction is approximately $13,125. The two-month delay adds an additional $26,250 in interest costs. By planning for delays and maintaining a cash reserve, Lisa is able to absorb this additional expense.

Once construction is complete, Lisa's restaurant generates $180,000 per month in revenue, with net income of $30,000 per month. Her loan is structured with a 25-year amortization, resulting in a monthly payment of approximately $16,000. After making her loan payment, Lisa has a net cash flow of $14,000 per month.

The property is appraised at $3,200,000 upon completion, creating immediate equity of $700,000. Over time, as the restaurant becomes more successful and property values increase, this equity grows. After five years, the property is valued at $3,800,000, and the loan balance is reduced to $2,000,000, giving Lisa $1,800,000 in equity.

Lisa's careful approach to risk management and cost control allows her to navigate challenges successfully and complete her project on solid financial footing. By planning for cost increases, managing delays, and maintaining financial discipline, she not only protects her investment but also positions herself for long-term growth and profitability.

Chapter 7

Maximizing Cash Flow and Profitability in SBA Construction and Expansion Projects

One of the most important goals of any SBA construction or expansion project is not simply completion—it is profitability. Building or expanding a commercial property is only successful if it generates strong, consistent cash flow while increasing long-term value. Many borrowers focus heavily on getting approved and completing construction but fail to optimize the financial performance of the asset once it is operational. SBA-backed financing through the U.S. Small Business Administration provides a powerful foundation, but maximizing cash flow requires strategy, planning, and ongoing management. This chapter focuses on how to turn your completed project into a high-performing, income-generating asset.

Cash flow is the lifeblood of any real estate or business investment. It is what allows you to cover expenses, service debt, reinvest in growth, and ultimately achieve financial freedom. In SBA construction projects, cash flow begins with proper planning during the early stages of development. This includes designing a property that supports revenue generation, selecting the right location, and structuring your financing in a way that keeps payments manageable. Every decision you make before and during construction impacts your ability to generate income after completion.

One of the most effective ways to maximize cash flow is through strategic property design. The layout and functionality of your building should be optimized for revenue generation. For example, designing flexible spaces that can be leased to multiple tenants allows you to diversify your income streams. Including additional features such as parking, storage areas, or shared amenities can also increase the value of the property and justify higher rents. A well-designed property not only attracts tenants or customers but also enhances operational efficiency, reducing costs over time.

Another key factor in maximizing profitability is understanding your revenue potential. This involves conducting a thorough market analysis to determine what similar properties are generating in terms of rent or business income. By setting competitive yet optimized pricing, you can maximize revenue without deterring demand. It is important to strike a balance—pricing too high may lead to vacancies, while pricing too low leaves money on the table. Continuous monitoring of market conditions allows you to adjust your strategy and maintain optimal performance.

Tenant mix plays a significant role in cash flow for multi-tenant properties. Selecting the right tenants can enhance the overall performance of your property. For example, complementary businesses can create synergy, attracting more customers and increasing foot traffic. A well-curated tenant mix not only improves income but also reduces risk by diversifying your revenue sources. Long-term leases with reliable tenants provide stability, while shorter-term leases offer flexibility to adjust rents as market conditions change.

Expense management is just as important as revenue generation. Controlling operating costs directly impacts your net income and overall profitability. This includes managing utilities, maintenance, property management fees, and other operational expenses. Implementing energy-efficient systems, negotiating favorable contracts, and maintaining the property proactively can significantly reduce costs. Even small reductions in expenses can have a substantial impact on long-term profitability.

Debt structure is another critical component of cash flow optimization. SBA loans typically offer long-term amortization, which helps keep monthly payments lower compared to shorter-term financing. However, understanding how your loan terms impact your cash flow is essential. This includes considering interest rates, repayment schedules, and potential refinancing opportunities. A well-structured loan aligns with your income, ensuring that debt service does not strain your finances.

Another powerful strategy for maximizing profitability is adding multiple income streams. In addition to primary revenue from your business or tenants, you can generate additional income through services, partnerships, or ancillary uses of the property. For example, leasing unused space, offering premium services, or incorporating complementary businesses can increase overall revenue. These additional streams enhance cash flow and make your property more resilient to changes in the market.

Operational efficiency is also key to profitability. Streamlining processes, implementing technology, and optimizing workflows can reduce costs and improve performance. For example, using property management software to track income and expenses allows you to identify inefficiencies and make data-driven decisions. Efficient operations not only improve profitability but also make your business easier to manage as it grows.

Another important concept is rent growth and income escalation. Over time, you should aim to increase your revenue through rent adjustments, improved services, or market appreciation. Including escalation clauses in leases allows you to increase rents gradually, keeping pace with inflation and market conditions. This ensures that your income continues to grow, enhancing both cash flow and property value.

Vacancy management is another critical factor. Vacant space represents lost income, so minimizing vacancies is essential to maintaining strong cash flow. This involves effective marketing, competitive pricing, and maintaining a high-quality property that attracts tenants. Building strong relationships with tenants also encourages retention, reducing turnover and associated costs.

Refinancing can also play a role in improving cash flow. Once your property has stabilized and increased in value, refinancing at a lower interest rate or longer term can reduce your monthly payments. This frees up additional cash flow that can be reinvested into your business or used for other opportunities. Understanding when and how to refinance is an important part of long-term profitability.

Another advanced strategy is leveraging appreciation. As your property increases in value, you gain equity that can be used to support additional investments. While appreciation does not directly impact monthly cash flow, it enhances your overall financial position and provides opportunities for growth. Combining cash flow with appreciation creates a powerful wealth-building strategy.

Ultimately, maximizing cash flow and profitability is about continuous improvement. It is not a one-time effort but an ongoing process of analyzing performance, identifying opportunities, and making strategic adjustments. By focusing on both revenue and expenses, optimizing your operations, and leveraging your financing effectively, you can transform your SBA construction project into a high-performing asset that generates consistent income and long-term value.

Real-Life Math Example: Maximizing Cash Flow in a Multi-Tenant Commercial Property

Consider a business owner named Rachel who completes an SBA-funded construction project for a 9,000-square-foot commercial building. The total project cost is $3,000,000, with a 10% down payment of $300,000 and a loan amount of $2,700,000 at a 7% interest rate over 25 years. Her monthly loan payment is approximately $19,000.

Rachel designs the building to include three separate units of 3,000 square feet each. She occupies one unit for her own business and leases the other two units to tenants. Each leased unit generates $12,000 per month in rent, resulting in total rental income of $24,000 per month.

Her business benefits from the new space, increasing its net income by $20,000 per month. This brings her total monthly income increase to $44,000. After subtracting operating expenses of $10,000 and the loan payment of $19,000, Rachel has a net cash flow of $15,000 per month.

To further increase profitability, Rachel implements additional strategies. She leases a portion of the parking area to a food truck vendor, generating an additional $1,500 per month. She also installs energy-efficient systems that reduce utility costs by $1,000 per month. These improvements increase her net cash flow to $17,500 per month.

Over time, Rachel increases rents by 3% annually. After three years, the rental income from the two units increases from $24,000 to approximately $26,200 per month. Her business income also grows, adding another $5,000 per month in net income. Her total monthly cash flow increases to over $23,000.

The property is appraised at $3,800,000 after stabilization, creating $800,000 in equity. Rachel refinances the property at a lower interest rate of 6%, reducing her monthly payment to

$17,000. This further increases her cash flow by $2,000 per month. Five years after completion, Rachel's property generates over $25,000 per month in net cash flow, while her equity has grown to over $1,500,000 due to appreciation and loan amortization. This strong financial performance allows her to reinvest in additional projects, continuing to grow her portfolio.

This example demonstrates how strategic planning, efficient operations, and continuous optimization can significantly enhance cash flow and profitability. By focusing on both revenue and expenses, Rachel transforms her SBA construction project into a high-performing asset that supports long-term financial success.

Chapter 8

Scaling Your Business Through SBA Construction and Expansion Strategies

Scaling a business is one of the most exciting yet challenging phases of entrepreneurship. Growth requires capital, planning, execution, and the ability to make strategic decisions that position your business for long-term success. SBA construction and expansion financing, supported by the U.S. Small Business Administration, provides a powerful framework for scaling operations in a structured and sustainable way. Unlike short-term growth strategies that rely on leasing or temporary solutions, SBA-backed expansion allows you to build permanent infrastructure, increase capacity, and create long-term value through real estate ownership. This chapter focuses on how to use these financing tools strategically to scale your business while maximizing profitability and minimizing risk.

Scaling through construction is fundamentally different from organic growth. Organic growth often relies on incremental increases in revenue, staffing, and operations, while construction-based scaling involves making a significant upfront investment to achieve a step-change in capacity and capability. This approach allows you to leap ahead of competitors, capture larger market share, and position your business as a dominant player in your industry. However, it also requires careful planning to ensure that the increased capacity translates into increased revenue. SBA financing provides the structure needed to support this type of growth, but the success of the strategy depends on how well it is executed.

One of the most important considerations in scaling through construction is timing. Expanding too early can strain your finances and lead to underutilized space, while expanding too late can result in missed opportunities and lost revenue. The key is to identify the point at which your current capacity is limiting your growth and to act before it becomes a bottleneck. This requires a deep understanding of your business metrics, including revenue trends, customer demand, and operational efficiency. By analyzing these factors, you can determine the optimal time to expand and ensure that your investment is aligned with your growth trajectory.

Another critical factor in scaling is location. The success of your expansion is heavily influenced by where you build or expand your property. Factors such as accessibility, visibility, market demand, and competition all play a role in determining the viability of your project. SBA lenders will also evaluate these factors during the approval process, as they directly impact the potential success of the project. Choosing the right location not only enhances your chances of approval but also increases the likelihood of achieving strong financial returns.

Design and functionality are also key components of successful scaling. When constructing or expanding a property, it is important to design the space in a way that supports your business operations and future growth. This includes optimizing layout, workflow, and customer experience. For example, a retail business may focus on maximizing foot traffic and display space, while a manufacturing facility may prioritize efficiency and scalability. By designing your property with growth in mind, you can avoid costly modifications in the future and ensure that your space continues to meet your needs as your business evolves.

Another powerful strategy for scaling is leveraging multi-use properties. SBA programs allow you to occupy a portion of the property while leasing out the remaining space. This creates an additional revenue stream that can offset your loan payments and improve your overall financial position. For example, a business owner might occupy 60% of a building and lease the remaining 40% to other tenants. This approach not only reduces your net occupancy cost but also diversifies your income, making your business more resilient to market fluctuations. Phased expansion is another effective strategy for managing growth. Instead of building a large facility all at once, you can expand in stages, allowing your business to grow gradually while minimizing risk. This approach enables you to generate revenue from completed portions of the project while continuing to build additional space. It also provides flexibility, allowing you to adjust your plans based on market conditions and business performance. SBA financing can be structured to support phased projects, making it easier to scale in a controlled and strategic manner.

Financing structure plays a crucial role in scaling success. SBA loans offer long-term amortization, lower down payments, and competitive interest rates, all of which contribute to improved cash flow. By structuring your loan effectively, you can ensure that your monthly payments remain manageable while still achieving significant growth. This includes considering factors such as loan term, interest rate, and repayment structure. A well-structured loan aligns with your business's cash flow, allowing you to reinvest profits into further growth.

Operational scalability is another important consideration. Expanding your physical space is only one part of the equation; you must also ensure that your operations can support increased capacity. This includes hiring and training staff, implementing efficient systems, and maintaining quality control. Without strong operational infrastructure, expansion can lead to inefficiencies and reduced profitability. SBA financing can include working capital to support these operational needs, ensuring that your business is prepared for growth.

Marketing and customer acquisition are also critical to scaling success. Increasing your capacity is only beneficial if you can fill that capacity with customers. This requires a strategic approach to marketing, including advertising, branding, and customer engagement. By aligning your marketing efforts with your expansion, you can ensure a steady flow of customers and maximize the return on your investment. SBA financing allows you to allocate resources to marketing and growth initiatives, further supporting your scaling strategy.

Another key benefit of scaling through SBA construction financing is equity creation. As you build or expand your property, you are not only increasing your business capacity but also creating a valuable asset. Over time, as the property appreciates and the loan balance decreases, your equity grows. This equity can be leveraged for future investments, additional expansions, or other financial opportunities. This dual benefit—business growth and wealth creation—is one of the most powerful aspects of SBA financing.

Risk management remains an important consideration when scaling. Larger projects involve greater complexity and potential challenges. By applying the principles of risk management discussed in previous chapters, you can mitigate these risks and ensure a successful outcome. This includes careful planning, selecting experienced professionals, and maintaining financial discipline throughout the project.

Ultimately, scaling your business through SBA construction and expansion financing is about creating a strategic pathway to growth. It requires vision, planning, and execution, but the rewards can be significant. By leveraging the advantages of SBA programs, you can build a strong foundation for your business, increase your capacity, and achieve long-term financial success. This chapter provides the strategies and insights needed to approach scaling with confidence and clarity, ensuring that your expansion is both effective and sustainable.

Real-Life Math Example: Scaling a Fitness Center Using SBA Construction Financing

Consider a business owner named Daniel who operates a successful fitness center generating $90,000 per month in revenue. Due to increasing demand, his current facility is at full capacity, and he is turning away potential customers. To scale his business, Daniel decides to construct a new, larger fitness center that will double his capacity and provide additional services such as personal training, group classes, and wellness programs. Daniel identifies a project with a total cost of $3,200,000. This includes $600,000 for land, $2,200,000 for construction, $200,000 for soft costs, and a $200,000 contingency reserve. He contributes a 10% down payment of $320,000, and the remaining $2,880,000 is financed through an SBA loan with a 25-year amortization at a 7% interest rate.

Daniel's monthly loan payment is approximately $20,400. To determine whether the project is financially viable, he analyzes the potential increase in revenue. By doubling his facility size and adding new services, he projects that his monthly revenue will increase from $90,000 to $180,000. After accounting for additional operating expenses, his net income is expected to increase from $25,000 to $55,000 per month.

After subtracting the loan payment of $20,400, Daniel's net cash flow is $34,600 per month. This represents a significant improvement over his previous cash flow and demonstrates the financial benefits of scaling through construction. Additionally, the property is appraised at $3,900,000 upon completion, creating immediate equity of $700,000.

Daniel also incorporates a multi-use strategy by leasing out a portion of the facility to a physical therapist and a nutrition consultant, generating an additional $5,000 per month in rental income. This further improves his cash flow and reduces his net occupancy cost. Over time, as his business continues to grow and property values increase, Daniel's equity position strengthens. After five years, the property is valued at $4,800,000, and the loan balance is reduced to $2,500,000, giving him $2,300,000 in equity. His monthly revenue has grown to $220,000, and his net income has increased accordingly.

This example illustrates how SBA construction financing can be used as a powerful tool for scaling a business. By making a strategic investment in expansion, Daniel was able to significantly increase his revenue, improve his cash flow, and build substantial equity. The key to his success was careful planning, effective execution, and a clear understanding of the financial impact of his decisions.

Chapter 9

Exit Strategies, Refinancing, and Long-Term Wealth Creation with SBA Construction Projects

Completing a construction or expansion project using SBA financing is a major milestone, but it is not the end of the journey—it is the beginning of long-term wealth creation. Many borrowers focus so heavily on getting approved and completing construction that they overlook one of the most important aspects of the entire process: the exit strategy. An exit strategy is not about leaving the investment; it is about maximizing its value, improving financial efficiency, and positioning yourself for future opportunities. SBA-backed projects supported by the U.S. Small Business Administration provide a powerful foundation for long-term growth, but the real wealth is built through strategic decisions made after the project is completed.

One of the most common and effective exit strategies is refinancing. While SBA loans offer excellent terms, including long amortization periods and relatively low down payments, there may come a time when refinancing into a conventional commercial loan makes financial sense. This is particularly true once the property has stabilized, increased in value, and demonstrated consistent cash flow. Refinancing can allow you to secure a lower interest rate, reduce monthly payments, or access equity for additional investments. Understanding when and how to refinance is critical to optimizing your financial position.

Timing plays a crucial role in refinancing decisions. Most SBA loans have prepayment penalties during the early years of the loan, which are designed to protect the lender's return. These penalties typically decrease over time, often structured as a declining percentage over the first 10 years. Waiting until these penalties are reduced or eliminated can significantly improve the financial benefits of refinancing. Additionally, refinancing is most effective when interest rates are favorable and the property has appreciated in value, creating additional equity.

Another important exit strategy is leveraging equity for expansion. As your property increases in value and your loan balance decreases, your equity grows. This equity can be accessed through refinancing or secondary financing, allowing you to fund new projects without needing to accumulate large amounts of cash. This strategy enables you to scale your portfolio more rapidly, using existing assets to generate new opportunities. For example, a business owner who has built significant equity in one property may use that equity to finance the construction of a second property, effectively multiplying their growth.

Selling the property is another potential exit strategy, particularly if the property has appreciated significantly or if market conditions are favorable. A well-executed SBA construction project can create substantial value, making the property attractive to investors or buyers. Selling allows you to realize this value and convert it into liquid capital, which can be reinvested into other opportunities. However, selling also means giving up future income and appreciation, so it is important to weigh the long-term benefits against the immediate gain.

A hybrid strategy that many experienced investors use is partial exit or repositioning. Instead of selling the entire property, you may choose to sell a portion, bring in partners, or refinance to extract equity while retaining ownership. This approach allows you to benefit from the property's value while still maintaining a stake in its future performance. It also provides flexibility, enabling you to adapt your strategy based on changing market conditions and personal goals.

Cash flow optimization is another key component of long-term wealth creation. Once your construction project is complete and operational, the focus shifts to maximizing income and minimizing expenses. This includes increasing rents, improving operational efficiency, and managing costs effectively. Even small improvements in cash flow can have a significant impact over time, particularly when combined with property appreciation and loan amortization. By continuously optimizing your property's performance, you can enhance its value and increase your overall return on investment.

Another powerful strategy is portfolio scaling. Instead of focusing on a single property, many borrowers use SBA construction financing as a starting point for building a portfolio of properties. Each successful project creates equity and cash flow that can be used to fund additional investments. Over time, this compounding effect can lead to substantial wealth accumulation. The key is to reinvest profits strategically and maintain financial discipline, ensuring that each new project is structured for success.

Tax advantages also play a significant role in long-term wealth creation. Real estate investments offer various tax benefits, including depreciation, interest deductions, and potential capital gains advantages. These benefits can significantly enhance your overall return and improve your financial position. Working with a qualified tax professional allows you to structure your investments in a way that maximizes these advantages while remaining compliant with regulations. Market timing and economic conditions are also important considerations in exit strategies. Real estate markets are cyclical, and understanding these cycles can help you make informed decisions about when to refinance, sell, or hold your property. For example, selling during a strong market may yield higher returns, while refinancing during periods of low interest rates can improve cash flow. Staying informed about market trends and economic indicators allows you to adapt your strategy and capitalize on opportunities.

Another advanced concept in exit strategy planning is legacy building. For many business owners and investors, the goal is not just to generate income but to create lasting wealth that can be passed down to future generations. SBA construction projects provide a tangible asset that can serve as a foundation for this legacy. By managing your properties effectively and making strategic decisions over time, you can build a portfolio that provides long-term financial security for your family.

Risk management remains important even in the exit phase. Decisions such as refinancing or selling should be based on careful analysis rather than short-term trends. Overleveraging, for example, can create financial strain, while selling too early may limit your long-term gains. Maintaining a balanced approach ensures that your decisions align with your overall financial goals and risk tolerance. Ultimately, exit strategies are about control and flexibility. They allow you to adapt to changing circumstances, optimize your financial position, and maximize the value of your investment. SBA construction financing provides the foundation, but it is your strategy that determines the outcome. By understanding the options available and making informed decisions, you can transform your project into a powerful engine for long-term wealth creation.

Real-Life Math Example: Refinancing and Wealth Creation from an SBA Construction Project

Consider a business owner named Robert who completed a commercial construction project using SBA financing. The total project cost was $3,000,000, with a 10% down payment of $300,000 and an SBA loan of $2,700,000 at a 7% interest rate with a 25-year amortization. His monthly payment is approximately $19,000.

After construction, the property generates $45,000 per month in net operating income. This results in a strong debt service coverage ratio, as the income significantly exceeds the loan payment. Over the first five years, Robert continues to operate the property successfully, increasing rents and improving efficiency. As a result, his net operating income grows to $55,000 per month. During this period, the property also appreciates in value. Initially appraised at $3,600,000 upon completion, it increases to $4,500,000 after five years. At the same time, Robert has paid down his loan balance to approximately $2,400,000. This gives him $2,100,000 in equity.

Robert decides to refinance the property into a conventional commercial loan at a lower interest rate of 6%. He refinances 70% of the property's value, which equals $3,150,000. After paying off the remaining SBA loan balance of $2,400,000, he receives $750,000 in cash from the refinance.

His new loan of $3,150,000 at 6% over 25 years results in a monthly payment of approximately $20,300. While this is slightly higher than his previous payment, his net operating income of $55,000 per month still provides strong cash flow. After the loan payment, he has $34,700 in monthly cash flow.

Robert uses the $750,000 from the refinance as a down payment for a second construction project. Assuming a similar structure with a 10% down payment, he is able to fund a new project worth $7,500,000. This significantly accelerates his growth and allows him to expand his portfolio.

Over time, Robert now owns two properties generating substantial income and equity. The first property continues to appreciate, while the second project follows a similar growth trajectory. After another five years, the combined value of both properties reaches $10,000,000, with total loan balances of $5,500,000, resulting in $4,500,000 in equity.

This example demonstrates how strategic refinancing and reinvestment can transform a single SBA construction project into a multi-property portfolio. By leveraging equity, optimizing cash flow, and making informed decisions, Robert is able to scale his investments and build long-term wealth.

Chapter 10

Advanced SBA Commercial Mortgage Loan Structuring for Complex Construction and Expansion Deals

As you progress beyond foundational SBA construction and expansion strategies, the next level of success comes from mastering advanced deal structuring. Complex SBA commercial mortgage structures allow experienced borrowers to optimize capital, reduce risk, accelerate growth, and create sophisticated real estate and business portfolios. While basic SBA loans provide access to funding, advanced structuring transforms that funding into a strategic financial engine. Supported by programs backed through the U.S. Small Business Administration, these structures give borrowers the flexibility to execute larger, multi-layered projects that combine construction, expansion, refinancing, and income generation into a single cohesive strategy.

At the advanced level, structuring is no longer just about getting approved—it is about designing a deal that performs at a high level over time. This involves aligning multiple components, including loan types, equity sources, cash flow strategies, and exit planning. Experienced borrowers often combine SBA 7(a) and SBA 504 structures with additional financing tools to create layered capital stacks. For example, a borrower may use SBA financing for the core real estate while incorporating seller financing, investor capital, or mezzanine financing to cover additional costs or reduce personal cash investment. This type of structuring requires a deep understanding of both financing options and risk management.

One of the most powerful advanced strategies is combining construction and acquisition into a single transaction. Instead of purchasing a property and then seeking separate financing for improvements, SBA loans can be structured to include acquisition, construction, equipment, and working capital in one package. This not only simplifies the process but also ensures that all components of the project are aligned from the beginning. By integrating these elements, borrowers can avoid the inefficiencies and risks associated with multiple financing stages.

Another key concept in advanced structuring is the use of special-purpose entities. Many experienced investors create separate legal entities for each project, allowing them to isolate risk and manage assets more effectively. This approach also provides flexibility in ownership structures, enabling partnerships and joint ventures. For example, a borrower may partner with investors who provide equity in exchange for a share of the project's profits. This reduces the borrower's financial burden while allowing them to control and execute the project.

Joint ventures and partnerships are particularly valuable in large or complex construction deals. By bringing in partners with complementary skills or capital, borrowers can undertake projects that would otherwise be beyond their reach. These partnerships must be carefully structured to ensure alignment of interests and clear responsibilities. This includes defining roles, profit distribution, and exit strategies. When done correctly, joint ventures can significantly enhance the scale and success of a project.

Another advanced technique is leveraging phased construction with strategic refinancing. Instead of completing a project all at once, borrowers may develop it in stages, refinancing each phase upon completion to unlock equity and fund subsequent phases. This approach allows for continuous growth without requiring large upfront capital. It also provides flexibility to adjust the project based on market conditions and performance. By combining construction financing with refinancing strategies, borrowers can create a cycle of development and reinvestment that accelerates portfolio growth. Cash flow engineering is another critical aspect of advanced structuring. This involves designing the project in a way that maximizes income and minimizes expenses. For example, incorporating multi-tenant spaces, leasing unused areas, or adding complementary businesses within the property can significantly increase revenue. Additionally, structuring lease agreements strategically can provide stable, predictable income that supports loan payments and enhances overall financial performance.

Advanced structuring also involves optimizing tax efficiency. Real estate investments offer numerous tax advantages, including depreciation, interest deductions, and potential deferral of capital gains through strategies such as exchanges. By working with tax professionals, borrowers can structure their projects in a way that maximizes these benefits and improves overall returns. Tax planning is not an afterthought—it is an integral part of the structuring process.

Risk diversification is another important consideration. Instead of concentrating all resources in a single project, advanced borrowers often diversify across multiple properties, locations, and asset types. This reduces exposure to market fluctuations and creates a more stable portfolio. For example, combining retail, office, and industrial properties can provide a balance of income streams and reduce overall risk. Another powerful strategy is incorporating value-add components into the project. This involves identifying opportunities to increase the property's value through improvements, repositioning, or operational enhancements. For example, renovating an outdated property, improving tenant mix, or adding new amenities can significantly increase income and property value. These value-add strategies are often the key to achieving higher returns and creating equity.

Exit strategy integration is essential in advanced structuring. Every deal should be designed with a clear exit plan, whether it involves refinancing, selling, or holding the property for long-term income. By considering the exit strategy from the beginning, borrowers can structure their deals to maximize flexibility and profitability. This includes understanding market conditions, timing, and potential buyer or investor demand.

Another advanced concept is leveraging credit and liquidity strategically. Experienced borrowers often maintain strong credit profiles and access to capital, allowing them to act quickly on opportunities. This includes using lines of credit, business credit, and other financial tools to support their projects. Maintaining liquidity ensures that borrowers can handle unexpected expenses and take advantage of new opportunities as they arise.

Ultimately, advanced SBA commercial mortgage loan structuring is about creating a system that supports continuous growth and wealth creation. It requires a combination of financial knowledge, strategic thinking, and disciplined execution. By mastering these techniques, borrowers can move beyond individual projects and build scalable, high-performing portfolios that generate long-term income and equity.

This chapter represents the culmination of the strategies outlined in this book. From understanding the basics of SBA construction financing to executing complex, multi-layered deals, you now have the tools to approach commercial real estate and business expansion with confidence. The key is to apply these principles consistently, adapt to changing conditions, and continue refining your strategy over time. With the right approach, SBA construction and expansion financing becomes more than a funding tool—it becomes a foundation for building a powerful and enduring financial future.

Real-Life Math Example: Advanced Structuring of a Multi-Phase Commercial Development

Consider an experienced investor named Sophia who plans to develop a multi-phase commercial property consisting of office space, retail units, and a small warehouse. The total projected cost for the full development is $10,000,000, but instead of building everything at once, Sophia decides to structure the project in phases to optimize capital and reduce risk. Phase 1 involves constructing a 10,000-square-foot office building at a cost of $4,000,000. Sophia contributes 10% equity, or $400,000, and finances the remaining $3,600,000 through an SBA loan at 7% interest with a 25-year amortization. Her monthly payment is approximately $25,500.

Upon completion, Phase 1 generates $60,000 per month in rental income, with net operating income of $40,000. After covering the loan payment, Sophia has $14,500 in monthly cash flow. The property is appraised at $5,200,000, creating $1,200,000 in equity.

Sophia then refinances Phase 1 at 70% of its new value, securing a loan of $3,640,000. After paying off the remaining SBA loan balance of $3,400,000, she receives $240,000 in cash. Combined with retained earnings from the property, she now has $500,000 available for Phase 2.

Phase 2 involves building retail units at a cost of $3,000,000. Using her $500,000 as equity, she finances the remaining $2,500,000 through another SBA loan. Upon completion, the retail units generate $45,000 per month in revenue, with net income of $30,000. The loan payment is approximately $17,700, resulting in $12,300 in monthly cash flow.

The combined value of Phases 1 and 2 is now $9,000,000, with total loan balances of approximately $6,000,000, giving Sophia $3,000,000 in equity. She then uses this equity to support Phase 3, which involves constructing a warehouse at a cost of $3,000,000.

After completing all three phases, the total property value reaches $12,500,000, with total loan balances of $8,000,000. This results in $4,500,000 in equity. The combined monthly net income from all phases is $85,000, while total loan payments are approximately $60,000, leaving $25,000 in monthly cash flow.

Over time, as rents increase and property values appreciate, Sophia's equity and cash flow continue to grow. After 10 years, the property value reaches $15,000,000, and loan balances are reduced to $6,000,000, resulting in $9,000,000 in equity.

This example demonstrates how advanced structuring techniques—such as phased development, refinancing, and reinvestment—can transform a single project into a large-scale, high-value portfolio. By leveraging SBA financing strategically, Sophia is able to scale her investments, maximize returns, and build substantial long-term wealth.

Chapter 11

Building a Long-Term SBA Construction Portfolio and Creating Generational Wealth

Reaching the stage where you are no longer focused on a single project but instead thinking in terms of a portfolio is a major transition in your journey as a business owner or real estate investor. At this level, SBA construction and expansion financing becomes more than a tool for individual deals—it becomes the foundation for a long-term system of wealth creation. Programs supported by the U.S. Small Business Administration allow you to build, expand, refinance, and scale properties in a structured way, but the real power lies in how you connect these projects into a cohesive portfolio strategy. This chapter focuses on how to build a portfolio that generates consistent income, grows in value over time, and ultimately creates generational wealth.

The first step in building a long-term portfolio is shifting your mindset from transactional thinking to strategic accumulation. Instead of viewing each project as a standalone opportunity, you begin to see each property as a building block within a larger system. Every construction project adds not only income but also equity, experience, and leverage that can be used for future deals. This compounding effect is what transforms individual investments into a powerful portfolio capable of producing long-term financial security.

A key principle in portfolio building is consistency. Rather than attempting to complete large, complex projects sporadically, successful investors focus on executing projects consistently over time. This approach allows you to refine your process, build relationships with lenders and contractors, and create a track record that improves your ability to secure financing. SBA lenders value experience and consistency, and as your portfolio grows, your credibility increases, making it easier to obtain approvals for larger and more complex deals.

Diversification is another critical component of a strong portfolio. While it may be tempting to focus on a single type of property or market, diversification reduces risk and creates multiple streams of income. For example, you might include office buildings, retail spaces, warehouses, and mixed-use properties within your portfolio. Each asset type responds differently to market conditions, providing stability and resilience. Geographic diversification can also be beneficial, allowing you to capitalize on opportunities in different markets and reduce exposure to localized economic downturns. Another important strategy is balancing owner-occupied and investment properties. SBA financing is primarily designed for owner-occupied businesses, but as your portfolio grows, you can strategically combine these with income-producing properties. For example, you might build a property for your own business while leasing out additional space, then use the equity and income from that property to support future investments. This hybrid approach allows you to meet SBA requirements while still building a diversified portfolio.

Equity growth is one of the most powerful drivers of portfolio expansion. Each time you complete a construction project, you create value by transforming land or an underutilized property into a higher-performing asset. As the property appreciates and the loan balance decreases, your equity increases. This equity can then be leveraged through refinancing or other financing strategies to fund additional projects. Over time, this creates a cycle of growth where each project supports the next, accelerating your portfolio expansion.

Cash flow is equally important in building a sustainable portfolio. While equity provides long-term value, cash flow ensures that your portfolio remains financially stable and capable of supporting itself. Properties that generate consistent income allow you to cover expenses, reinvest in new opportunities, and weather economic fluctuations. Balancing equity growth with cash flow is essential to maintaining a healthy portfolio.

Another key aspect of portfolio building is operational efficiency. As your portfolio grows, managing multiple properties becomes increasingly complex. Implementing systems and processes for property management, accounting, and maintenance ensures that your operations remain efficient and scalable. This may involve hiring property managers, using technology to track performance, and standardizing procedures across your portfolio. Efficient operations not only reduce costs but also improve overall performance.

Financing strategy plays a central role in portfolio growth. SBA loans provide an excellent starting point, but as your portfolio expands, you may incorporate additional financing options, including conventional loans, private financing, and lines of credit. Understanding how to combine these tools allows you to optimize your capital structure and maintain flexibility. This includes knowing when to use SBA financing and when to transition to other types of funding based on your goals and the characteristics of each project.

Long-term planning is essential for creating generational wealth. This involves not only building your portfolio but also structuring it in a way that can be passed down to future generations. This may include estate planning, creating legal entities, and establishing clear ownership structures. By planning for the future, you can ensure that your portfolio continues to provide value and stability for your family.

Another important consideration is market awareness. Real estate markets are constantly evolving, and staying informed about trends, opportunities, and risks is essential to making informed decisions. This includes monitoring economic indicators, understanding supply and demand dynamics, and identifying emerging markets. By staying ahead of market trends, you can position your portfolio to capitalize on opportunities and avoid potential pitfalls.

Risk management remains a critical component of portfolio building. While diversification reduces risk, it does not eliminate it. Each property and market carries its own set of challenges, and managing these risks requires careful planning and ongoing monitoring. This includes maintaining adequate reserves, ensuring proper insurance coverage, and continuously evaluating the performance of your portfolio.

Another advanced concept in portfolio building is scaling through partnerships. As your portfolio grows, you may choose to partner with other investors to access additional capital and expertise. These partnerships can enable you to undertake larger projects and expand more rapidly. However, they must be structured carefully to ensure alignment of interests and clear expectations.

Ultimately, building a long-term SBA construction portfolio is about creating a system that generates income, builds equity, and supports continuous growth. It requires discipline, strategic thinking, and a commitment to long-term success. By applying the principles outlined in this chapter, you can transform individual projects into a powerful portfolio that provides financial security, flexibility, and the foundation for generational wealth.

Real-Life Math Example: Building a Multi-Property SBA Construction Portfolio Over 10 Years

Consider an investor named Michael who begins with a single SBA construction project. His first project is a small office building with a total cost of $2,000,000. He contributes a 10% down payment of $200,000 and finances the remaining $1,800,000 through an SBA loan at 7% interest over 25 years. His monthly payment is approximately $12,700.

The property generates $25,000 per month in net operating income, resulting in a monthly cash flow of $12,300 after debt service. Over the first three years, the property appreciates to $2,600,000, and the loan balance decreases to $1,700,000, giving Michael $900,000 in equity. Michael refinances the property at 70% of its value, securing a new loan of $1,820,000. After paying off the remaining SBA balance, he receives $120,000 in cash. Combined with his savings from cash flow, he now has $300,000 to invest in a second project.

The second project is a retail property with a total cost of $3,000,000. Michael uses his $300,000 as a 10% down payment and finances the remaining $2,700,000. This property generates $40,000 per month in net operating income, with a loan payment of approximately $19,000, resulting in $21,000 in monthly cash flow.

After five years, Michael owns two properties with a combined value of $6,500,000 and total loan balances of $4,000,000, giving him $2,500,000 in equity. His combined monthly cash flow is approximately $33,000.

Michael continues this strategy, using equity and cash flow to fund additional projects. By year 10, he owns five properties with a combined value of $15,000,000. His total loan balances are $9,000,000, resulting in $6,000,000 in equity. His portfolio generates $120,000 per month in net operating income, with total loan payments of $65,000, leaving $55,000 in monthly cash flow.

This portfolio provides Michael with significant financial flexibility. He can reinvest in additional properties, pay down debt, or use the income to support his lifestyle. Over time, as loans are paid off and properties continue to appreciate, his wealth continues to grow.

This example demonstrates how consistent execution, strategic refinancing, and disciplined reinvestment can transform a single SBA construction project into a substantial portfolio. By leveraging the principles outlined in this chapter, Michael is able to build long-term wealth and create a financial legacy for future generations.

Chapter 12

Putting It All Together — Your Complete SBA Construction and Expansion Blueprint

At this point in your journey through SBA construction and expansion financing, you have learned how to identify opportunities, structure deals, secure approval, manage construction, control risk, scale strategically, and build a long-term portfolio. This final chapter is about bringing all of those elements together into a clear, repeatable blueprint that you can use to execute projects with confidence and consistency. SBA-backed financing through the U.S. Small Business Administration is not just a one-time opportunity—it is a system that, when used correctly, can support continuous growth, financial stability, and long-term wealth creation.

The first step in your blueprint is clarity of vision. Every successful project begins with a clear understanding of what you want to achieve. This includes defining your business goals, identifying the type of property you want to build or expand, and understanding how the project will generate income. Without a clear vision, it becomes difficult to make strategic decisions or communicate effectively with lenders, contractors, and partners. Your vision serves as the foundation for every step that follows, guiding your planning, financing, and execution.

Once your vision is established, the next step is opportunity selection. Not every project is worth pursuing, and one of the most important skills you can develop is the ability to identify high-quality opportunities. This involves analyzing market demand, location, competition, and potential revenue. A strong opportunity is one that aligns with your goals, meets lender requirements, and has the potential to generate consistent income. By focusing on quality over quantity, you can reduce risk and increase your chances of success.

The third step in the blueprint is deal structuring. As you learned in earlier chapters, how you structure your loan has a significant impact on your project's performance. This includes determining the appropriate loan program, calculating your equity injection, and ensuring that your projected income supports the loan payments. A well-structured deal balances affordability, risk, and growth potential, creating a strong foundation for execution.

After structuring the deal, the next step is preparing for approval. This involves assembling a comprehensive loan package that includes financial statements, tax returns, business plans, construction budgets, and projections. The goal is to present a clear and compelling case to the lender, demonstrating that your project is viable and that you have the capacity to execute it successfully. Preparation is key—well-organized documentation and realistic projections can significantly improve your chances of approval.

Once approved, the focus shifts to execution. Managing the construction process effectively is critical to the success of your project. This includes coordinating with contractors, managing the draw schedule, and ensuring that the project stays on time and within budget. Execution requires attention to detail, strong communication, and the ability to adapt to challenges as they arise. By maintaining control over the process, you can ensure that your project is completed successfully.

Risk management is integrated throughout the entire blueprint. From budgeting and contractor selection to contingency planning and compliance, managing risk is essential at every stage of the project. By anticipating potential challenges and developing strategies to address them, you can minimize disruptions and protect your investment. Risk management is not about avoiding challenges—it is about being prepared to handle them effectively.

Another critical component of the blueprint is financial management. This includes tracking expenses, managing cash flow, and ensuring that your project remains financially viable. Understanding your numbers allows you to make informed decisions and adjust your strategy as needed. Financial discipline is what separates successful projects from those that struggle or fail.

As your project reaches completion, the blueprint transitions into optimization. This involves maximizing the performance of your property by increasing income, reducing expenses, and improving operational efficiency. Whether through leasing additional space, enhancing customer experience, or streamlining operations, optimization ensures that your property delivers the highest possible return.

Refinancing and equity leverage are the next steps in the blueprint. Once your property has stabilized and increased in value, you can use refinancing to access equity and fund additional projects. This creates a cycle of growth where each project supports the next. By leveraging your assets strategically, you can scale your portfolio and accelerate wealth creation.

Portfolio building is the long-term goal of the blueprint. Instead of focusing on individual projects, you begin to think in terms of a system of assets that generate income and appreciate over time. Each project becomes a building block within a larger portfolio, creating multiple streams of income and increasing your overall financial stability. This shift in perspective is what transforms short-term success into long-term wealth.

Another important element of the blueprint is continuous improvement. Every project provides valuable experience and insights that can be applied to future deals. By analyzing your performance, identifying areas for improvement, and refining your strategy, you can continuously enhance your results. This commitment to growth ensures that your projects become more efficient and profitable over time.

Partnerships and relationships also play a key role in the blueprint. Building strong relationships with lenders, contractors, and advisors creates a support network that can help you navigate challenges and identify new opportunities. These relationships become increasingly valuable as your portfolio grows, providing access to resources and expertise that support your success.

Ultimately, this blueprint is about creating a repeatable system for success. It provides a clear path from vision to execution to growth, allowing you to approach each project with confidence and clarity. By following this blueprint, you can transform SBA construction and expansion financing into a powerful tool for achieving your financial goals and building long-term wealth.

This final chapter represents the culmination of everything you have learned in this series. It is not just about understanding the concepts—it is about applying them consistently and strategically. With the right mindset, planning, and execution, you can use SBA financing to build, expand, and scale your business while creating a lasting financial legacy.

Real-Life Math Example: Applying the Full SBA Construction Blueprint to Build a Scalable Portfolio

Consider an entrepreneur named Kevin who follows this blueprint to build a scalable portfolio over time. Kevin begins with a clear vision: to own and operate a series of mixed-use commercial properties that generate both business income and rental revenue.

His first project is a small mixed-use building with a total cost of $2,500,000. He contributes a 10% down payment of $250,000 and finances the remaining $2,250,000 through an SBA loan at 7% interest over 25 years. His monthly payment is approximately $16,000.

The property generates $35,000 per month in net operating income, resulting in $19,000 in monthly cash flow after debt service. Over the first three years, the property appreciates to $3,200,000, and Kevin pays down the loan balance to $2,100,000, giving him $1,100,000 in equity.

Kevin refinances the property at 70% of its value, securing a new loan of $2,240,000. After paying off the existing loan, he receives $140,000 in cash. Combined with savings from cash flow, he now has $400,000 to invest in a second project.

The second project costs $4,000,000, with Kevin contributing $400,000 as a down payment. The property generates $55,000 per month in net operating income, with a loan payment of approximately $28,000, resulting in $27,000 in monthly cash flow.

After five years, Kevin owns two properties with a combined value of $7,500,000 and loan balances of $5,000,000, giving him $2,500,000 in equity. His combined monthly cash flow is $46,000.

Kevin continues to apply the blueprint, using equity and cash flow to fund additional projects. By year 10, he owns four properties with a combined value of $14,000,000. His total loan balances are $8,500,000, resulting in $5,500,000 in equity. His portfolio generates $110,000 per month in net operating income, with loan payments of $65,000, leaving $45,000 in monthly cash flow.

Kevin's disciplined approach allows him to scale his portfolio while maintaining strong financial performance. By following a structured blueprint, he is able to manage risk, optimize cash flow, and build substantial equity over time.

This example illustrates how applying a repeatable system can transform individual projects into a scalable portfolio. By combining strategic planning, effective execution, and continuous improvement, Kevin creates a sustainable path to long-term wealth and financial independence.

Chapter 13

Scaling Beyond SBA Limits – Transitioning to Advanced Commercial Financing and Building an Empire

As you successfully execute multiple SBA construction and expansion projects, there comes a point where your growth begins to outpace the natural limits of SBA financing. While SBA programs backed by the U.S. Small Business Administration are incredibly powerful for building a strong foundation, they are not designed to support unlimited scale. Loan caps, owner-occupancy requirements, and program guidelines eventually create boundaries that advanced investors must learn to navigate. This chapter focuses on how to transition beyond SBA financing while still leveraging the knowledge, equity, and systems you have built to create a larger, more sophisticated commercial real estate empire.

The first step in scaling beyond SBA limits is recognizing when you are approaching those limits. SBA loan caps, typically in the range of several million dollars depending on the program, can restrict the size and number of projects you can undertake. Additionally, the requirement for owner occupancy limits the ability to pursue purely investment-based properties. As your portfolio grows and your ambitions expand, you may find that these constraints no longer align with your goals. This is not a limitation—it is a signal that you are ready to move into the next phase of growth.

Transitioning beyond SBA financing begins with understanding alternative funding sources. Conventional commercial loans, portfolio loans from banks, private lenders, and institutional financing all provide opportunities to scale your investments. Unlike SBA loans, these options often focus more heavily on the performance of the property and less on owner occupancy. This opens the door to a wider range of opportunities, including multi-tenant investment properties, large-scale developments, and mixed-use projects. By expanding your financing toolkit, you gain the flexibility to pursue larger and more diverse investments.

One of the most important advantages you bring into this transition is your track record. Lenders outside of the SBA system place significant value on experience and performance. Your history of successfully completing SBA construction projects, managing properties, and generating cash flow becomes a powerful asset. It demonstrates your ability to execute complex deals and reduces perceived risk. This credibility can lead to better loan terms, higher leverage, and access to larger amounts of capital. Another key strategy in scaling beyond SBA limits is leveraging partnerships. As projects become larger and more complex, it often makes sense to bring in partners who can contribute capital, expertise, or both. These partnerships can take many forms, including joint ventures, syndications, and equity partnerships. By sharing resources and responsibilities, you can undertake projects that would be difficult or impossible to execute on your own. However, structuring these partnerships requires careful planning to ensure alignment of interests and clear communication.

Capital stacking becomes increasingly important as you move into larger deals. This involves combining multiple sources of financing to fund a project. For example, you might use a conventional loan for a portion of the project, equity from investors for another portion, and mezzanine financing to fill any gaps. This layered approach allows you to maximize leverage while maintaining control over the project. Understanding how to structure these capital stacks is a key skill for advanced investors.

Another critical concept is scaling through systems. As your portfolio grows, managing multiple projects and properties becomes more complex. Developing systems for deal analysis, project management, financial tracking, and property management allows you to operate efficiently at scale. This may involve using technology, hiring specialized staff, and standardizing processes across your portfolio. Systems are what enable you to move from being an operator to being a true business owner and investor.

Portfolio optimization is also essential in this phase. Instead of simply adding more properties, you begin to focus on improving the performance of your existing assets. This includes increasing rents, reducing expenses, and repositioning properties to maximize value. By optimizing your portfolio, you can increase cash flow and equity without necessarily acquiring new properties. This creates a strong financial foundation that supports further growth.

Another advanced strategy is geographic expansion. While your initial projects may have been concentrated in a single market, expanding into new regions allows you to access additional opportunities and diversify risk. Different markets offer different advantages, including varying levels of demand, pricing, and growth potential. By carefully selecting new markets, you can enhance your portfolio's performance and resilience.

Institutional thinking is another key element of scaling beyond SBA limits. This involves approaching your investments with a long-term, strategic mindset similar to that of large real estate firms. Instead of focusing on individual deals, you begin to think in terms of portfolio performance, capital allocation, and risk management. This shift in perspective allows you to make more informed decisions and position your portfolio for sustained growth.

Debt management becomes increasingly important as your portfolio grows. While leverage is a powerful tool, it must be used carefully to avoid overexposure. Maintaining a balanced debt structure, with manageable payments and sufficient cash flow, ensures that your portfolio remains stable even during economic downturns. This includes monitoring interest rates, refinancing strategically, and maintaining adequate reserves.

Another important consideration is branding and reputation. As you transition into larger and more complex deals, your reputation becomes a valuable asset. Building a strong brand as a reliable and successful investor can open doors to new opportunities, partnerships, and financing options. This includes maintaining professionalism, delivering on commitments, and building strong relationships within the industry.

Exit strategies also evolve at this level. Instead of focusing solely on individual property exits, you may consider portfolio-level strategies, such as selling a group of properties, bringing in institutional investors, or even creating a real estate fund. These strategies allow you to realize the value of your portfolio at a higher level and provide opportunities for significant financial gains.

Ultimately, scaling beyond SBA limits is about transitioning from building projects to building an empire. It requires a combination of financial knowledge, strategic thinking, and disciplined execution. The foundation you have built through SBA construction financing provides the skills, experience, and assets needed to succeed at this level. By expanding your approach and embracing advanced strategies, you can continue to grow your portfolio and achieve your long-term goals.

This chapter represents the next step in your evolution as an investor. It is about taking everything you have learned and applying it on a larger scale. With the right mindset and strategy, the transition beyond SBA financing is not an end—it is a beginning. It is the point where your growth accelerates, your opportunities expand, and your vision becomes reality on a much larger scale.

Real-Life Math Example: Transitioning from SBA Projects to a Large-Scale Commercial Portfolio

Consider an investor named Olivia who has successfully completed three SBA construction projects. Each project averaged $3,000,000 in total cost, resulting in a combined portfolio value of $9,000,000. After several years of appreciation and loan amortization, her portfolio is now valued at $12,000,000, with total loan balances of $7,000,000. This gives her $5,000,000 in equity.

Olivia wants to scale beyond SBA limits and pursue a larger commercial development project valued at $15,000,000. Instead of relying solely on SBA financing, she structures a capital stack that includes a conventional loan covering 65% of the project ($9,750,000), equity from investors covering 25% ($3,750,000), and her own contribution of $1,500,000, which she sources from refinancing her existing properties.

The conventional loan is structured at a 6.5% interest rate over 25 years, resulting in a monthly payment of approximately $65,800. The project is designed to generate $140,000 per month in net operating income once stabilized. After covering the loan payment, Olivia and her investors share $74,200 in monthly cash flow.

Olivia retains a 50% ownership stake in the project, giving her $37,100 in monthly cash flow from this development alone. Combined with the income from her existing portfolio, her total monthly cash flow exceeds $80,000. Over the next five years, the new development appreciates to $18,000,000, while the loan balance decreases to $8,500,000. Olivia's share of equity in the project is now $4,750,000. Combined with her existing portfolio, her total equity exceeds $10,000,000.

This transition allows Olivia to move from small to mid-sized projects into large-scale developments. By leveraging her SBA experience, using advanced financing structures, and partnering with investors, she is able to significantly increase her scale and financial returns.

This example demonstrates how the transition beyond SBA financing can unlock new levels of growth. By combining experience, equity, and strategic structuring, Olivia transforms her portfolio into a large-scale operation capable of generating substantial income and long-term wealth.

Chapter 14

Mastering Deal Flow, Lead Generation, and Finding High-Profit SBA Construction Opportunities

At the highest level of success in SBA construction and expansion financing, the challenge is no longer understanding how to structure a deal or manage a project—it is consistently finding high-quality opportunities. The ability to generate deal flow is what separates average investors from those who build powerful, scalable portfolios. SBA-backed financing through the U.S. Small Business Administration provides the tools to execute deals, but without a steady pipeline of opportunities, growth becomes limited. This chapter focuses on how to create a system for identifying, evaluating, and securing high-profit construction and expansion deals on a consistent basis.

Deal flow is the lifeblood of any real estate or business expansion strategy. It refers to the continuous stream of opportunities that you analyze and potentially pursue. The more opportunities you have access to, the more selective you can be, and the higher the quality of the deals you ultimately execute. Instead of chasing deals sporadically, successful investors build systems that attract opportunities to them.

This shift—from reactive to proactive—transforms your ability to scale.

One of the most effective ways to generate deal flow is through relationships. Building strong relationships with real estate agents, brokers, lenders, contractors, and other professionals creates a network that can provide access to opportunities before they become widely available. Many of the best deals are never listed publicly—they are shared within networks of trusted professionals. By positioning yourself as a serious and capable investor, you can become the first person people think of when opportunities arise.

Direct outreach is another powerful strategy. Instead of waiting for opportunities to come to you, you can actively seek out potential deals by contacting property owners, business owners, and developers. This may involve calling, emailing, or sending targeted marketing messages to individuals who own properties that fit your criteria. For example, you might target owners of underutilized commercial properties, outdated buildings, or businesses that are outgrowing their current space. By identifying these opportunities early, you can structure deals that create significant value.

Digital marketing and data-driven strategies are increasingly important in generating deal flow. Platforms that provide property data, market insights, and owner information allow you to identify potential opportunities with precision. By analyzing data such as property values, ownership history, and market trends, you can target properties that are most likely to benefit from construction or expansion. Combining this data with targeted marketing campaigns allows you to reach potential sellers and partners efficiently.

Another effective strategy is focusing on niche markets. Instead of competing for highly visible, competitive deals, you can specialize in specific types of properties or industries. For example, you might focus on medical offices, warehouses, childcare facilities, or mixed-use developments. By becoming an expert in a particular niche, you can identify opportunities that others overlook and create value through specialized knowledge.

Value-add opportunities are particularly attractive in SBA construction and expansion projects. These are properties or businesses that have the potential for improvement through renovation, expansion, or repositioning. For example, an outdated building in a growing area may have significant upside potential if renovated or expanded. Similarly, a business operating in a small space may benefit from moving into a larger, purpose-built facility. Identifying these opportunities requires a combination of market knowledge, creativity, and financial analysis.

Deal analysis is a critical component of the deal flow process. Not every opportunity is worth pursuing, and the ability to evaluate deals quickly and accurately is essential. This includes analyzing costs, projected income, market conditions, and potential risks. By developing a consistent framework for evaluating deals, you can make informed decisions and focus your time and resources on the most promising opportunities.

Speed is another important factor in securing deals. In competitive markets, the ability to act quickly can make the difference between winning and losing a deal. This requires having your financing, team, and processes in place so that you can move forward without delays. SBA financing may take time to close, but demonstrating readiness and commitment can give you an advantage in negotiations.

Another key strategy is creating multiple entry points for opportunities. This means generating deals from various sources, including brokers, direct outreach, online platforms, and referrals. By diversifying your deal flow sources, you reduce reliance on any single channel and increase the likelihood of finding high-quality opportunities.

Building a brand is also an important aspect of deal flow. As your reputation grows, more opportunities will come to you organically. This includes being known as someone who can close deals, execute projects, and deliver results. A strong brand attracts not only deals but also partners, investors, and lenders who want to work with you.

Another advanced concept is creating deal flow through partnerships. By collaborating with other investors, developers, or business owners, you can access opportunities that you might not find on your own. These partnerships can also allow you to share resources and expertise, making it easier to execute larger or more complex projects.

Consistency is the key to long-term success in deal flow. Generating opportunities is not a one-time effort—it requires ongoing activity and commitment. This includes regularly reaching out to contacts, analyzing deals, and refining your strategy. Over time, this consistency builds momentum, creating a steady pipeline of opportunities that supports continuous growth.

Ultimately, mastering deal flow is about creating a system that works for you. It is about combining relationships, data, marketing, and analysis into a cohesive strategy that consistently produces high-quality opportunities. SBA construction and expansion financing provides the foundation, but deal flow is what drives growth. By mastering this aspect of your business, you can unlock the full potential of your strategy and achieve sustained success.

Real-Life Math Example: Building Deal Flow and Identifying a High-Profit SBA Construction Opportunity

Consider an investor named Carlos who has developed a system for generating deal flow. Through a combination of broker relationships, direct outreach, and data analysis, he reviews 20 potential opportunities each month. Out of these, he identifies two deals that meet his criteria and performs a detailed analysis on each.

One of these opportunities involves a 1-acre property with an outdated commercial building priced at $800,000. Carlos determines that the existing building can be demolished and replaced with a new 8,000-square-foot mixed-use development. The estimated construction cost is $1,600,000, with $200,000 in soft costs and a $200,000 contingency reserve. This brings the total project cost to $2,800,000.

Using SBA financing, Carlos contributes a 10% down payment of $280,000 and finances the remaining $2,520,000. The loan is structured at a 7% interest rate over 25 years, resulting in a monthly payment of approximately $17,900.

Carlos projects that the completed property will generate $50,000 per month in rental income, with net operating income of $35,000 after expenses. After subtracting the loan payment, he achieves a net cash flow of $17,100 per month.

The property is appraised at $3,600,000 upon completion, creating immediate equity of $800,000. This represents a significant increase from the total project cost and demonstrates the value created through construction and repositioning.

Carlos continues to generate deal flow and completes two similar projects over the next three years. Each project follows a similar structure, resulting in a portfolio valued at $10,000,000 with total loan balances of $6,500,000. This gives him $3,500,000 in equity and combined monthly cash flow of $45,000.

By consistently generating and analyzing opportunities, Carlos is able to identify high-profit deals and execute them effectively. His system allows him to focus on the best opportunities while maintaining a steady pipeline of potential projects.

This example demonstrates the importance of deal flow in scaling a portfolio. By reviewing multiple opportunities, applying disciplined analysis, and executing high-quality deals, Carlos is able to build significant wealth and create a sustainable growth strategy.

Chapter 15

Building Your SBA Construction Legacy — From Deals to a Lasting Financial Empire

At the highest level of SBA construction and expansion financing, success is no longer defined by individual deals, properties, or even portfolios—it is defined by the legacy you create. The journey from your first SBA-funded project to a fully scaled operation supported by the U.S. Small Business Administration is about more than financial gain. It is about building a system that produces consistent income, appreciates in value, and can be sustained and passed down over generations. This chapter is about shifting your focus from short-term wins to long-term impact, transforming your strategy into a lasting financial empire.

A legacy is built on consistency, discipline, and vision. While many investors achieve success with a few projects, only a small percentage are able to sustain and grow that success over decades. The difference lies in their approach. Instead of chasing deals, they build systems. Instead of focusing on immediate returns, they focus on long-term growth. Every decision is made with the future in mind, ensuring that their portfolio continues to perform and expand over time.

The first component of building a legacy is creating a scalable system. This means developing processes for deal flow, financing, construction management, and property operations that can be replicated across multiple projects. A scalable system allows you to move beyond being directly involved in every detail and instead focus on strategic decision-making. This includes building a team, leveraging technology, and standardizing workflows. When your system is strong, your growth becomes more predictable and sustainable.

Another critical element is leadership. As your portfolio grows, your role evolves from operator to leader. You are no longer just managing projects—you are guiding a team, making strategic decisions, and setting the direction for your business. This requires strong leadership skills, including communication, delegation, and the ability to inspire others. Building a capable team allows you to scale more effectively and ensures that your operations run smoothly.

Financial discipline remains at the core of your legacy. Regardless of how large your portfolio becomes, maintaining control over your finances is essential. This includes managing debt responsibly, maintaining adequate reserves, and continuously monitoring the performance of your properties.

Financial discipline ensures that your portfolio remains stable and resilient, even during challenging economic conditions.

Another key aspect of building a legacy is reinvestment. Instead of consuming all of your profits, you reinvest a portion back into your portfolio to fuel further growth. This creates a compounding effect, where each project contributes to the next. Over time, this compounding can lead to exponential growth, significantly increasing your wealth and financial stability.

Brand and reputation are also essential components of a lasting legacy. As you complete projects and build your portfolio, your reputation becomes a valuable asset. Being known as a reliable, professional, and successful investor attracts opportunities, partners, and capital. Your brand is not just about marketing—it is about the trust and credibility you build within your industry.

Another important consideration is succession planning. A true legacy extends beyond your lifetime, and this requires planning for how your portfolio will be managed and transferred in the future. This may involve creating legal structures, establishing trusts, or training the next generation to take over your business. By planning ahead, you can ensure that your legacy continues to provide value and stability for years to come. Diversification continues to play a role in long-term success. A well-diversified portfolio reduces risk and provides multiple streams of income. This includes diversifying across property types, markets, and income sources. By spreading your investments strategically, you create a more stable and resilient portfolio that can withstand market fluctuations.

Another advanced concept is vertical integration. As your portfolio grows, you may choose to bring certain functions in-house, such as property management, construction management, or even financing. This allows you to control more aspects of your business, reduce costs, and improve efficiency. Vertical integration can significantly enhance your profitability and give you a competitive advantage.

Innovation is also important in maintaining a long-term legacy. Markets evolve, technologies change, and new opportunities emerge. Staying adaptable and open to new ideas allows you to remain competitive and continue growing. This includes adopting new technologies, exploring new markets, and continuously refining your strategy.

Another powerful element of a legacy is impact. Beyond financial success, your projects can have a positive impact on communities, businesses, and individuals. By creating spaces that support economic growth, provide jobs, and improve quality of life, you contribute to something larger than yourself. This impact becomes part of your legacy, adding meaning and purpose to your work.

Long-term wealth creation is not just about accumulation—it is about preservation. Protecting your assets through proper legal structures, insurance, and risk management ensures that your portfolio remains intact and continues to perform. This includes safeguarding against potential liabilities and maintaining compliance with regulations.

Ultimately, building your SBA construction legacy is about creating a system that endures. It is about turning your knowledge, experience, and resources into a sustainable operation that continues to grow and evolve. This requires vision, discipline, and a commitment to long-term success.

As you reflect on everything you have learned throughout this series, you now have the tools to move from individual projects to a fully developed empire. SBA construction and expansion financing has provided the foundation, but it is your strategy and execution that determine the outcome. By applying these principles consistently, you can build a legacy that not only achieves financial success but also creates lasting value for generations to come.

Real-Life Math Example: Building a Long-Term Legacy Through SBA Construction Projects

Consider an investor named Anthony who begins his journey with a single SBA construction project. His first project is a small commercial building with a total cost of $2,000,000. He contributes a 10% down payment of $200,000 and finances the remaining $1,800,000 through an SBA loan at 7% interest over 25 years. His monthly payment is approximately $12,700.

The property generates $28,000 per month in net operating income, resulting in $15,300 in monthly cash flow after debt service. Anthony reinvests a portion of this cash flow while saving the rest. Over the first three years, the property appreciates to $2,600,000, and the loan balance decreases to $1,700,000, giving him $900,000 in equity.

Anthony refinances the property at 70% of its value, securing a new loan of $1,820,000. After paying off the existing loan, he receives $120,000 in cash. Combined with his savings, he now has $350,000 to invest in a second project.

The second project costs $3,500,000 and generates $45,000 per month in net operating income. After debt service, Anthony earns $20,000 in monthly cash flow. Over time, he repeats this process, using equity and cash flow to fund additional projects. After 10 years, Anthony owns six properties with a combined value of $18,000,000. His total loan balances are $10,500,000, resulting in $7,500,000 in equity. His portfolio generates $140,000 per month in net operating income, with loan payments of $80,000, leaving $60,000 in monthly cash flow.

Anthony implements a succession plan, creating a trust to manage his properties and ensure that they are passed down to his family. He also builds a management team to oversee operations, allowing him to focus on strategic growth.

Over the next decade, his portfolio continues to grow and appreciate. By year 20, the total value of his properties reaches $30,000,000, with loan balances reduced to $8,000,000, resulting in $22,000,000 in equity. His monthly cash flow exceeds $120,000, providing financial security and flexibility.

This example illustrates how consistent reinvestment, disciplined financial management, and strategic planning can transform a single SBA construction project into a lasting financial legacy. By focusing on long-term growth and sustainability, Anthony builds an empire that continues to generate income and create wealth for future generations.

Closing Thoughts

The SBA Construction and Expansion Advantage

As you reach the end of this journey through SBA construction and expansion financing, it is important to recognize that what you have gained is far more than knowledge about loans, projects, or real estate. You have developed a framework for thinking differently about growth, opportunity, and wealth creation. The strategies, systems, and insights outlined throughout this series are designed to empower you to take control of your financial future, using tools supported by the U.S. Small Business Administration as a foundation for building something meaningful and lasting.

The true power of SBA construction financing lies in its ability to turn vision into reality. Many people have ideas for businesses, expansions, or real estate developments, but they lack the capital or structure to execute them. SBA programs bridge that gap, providing access to financing that would otherwise be difficult to obtain. However, access alone is not enough. The difference between those who succeed and those who struggle is how they apply what they have learned. Execution is everything, and your ability to take action will determine your results. Throughout this series, you have seen how each stage of the process builds upon the last. From understanding the fundamentals to structuring deals, securing approval, managing construction, controlling risk, scaling operations, and building a portfolio, each step is part of a larger system. This system is designed to be repeatable, allowing you to move from one project to the next with increasing confidence and efficiency. Over time, this repetition creates momentum, and that momentum becomes the driving force behind your growth.

One of the most important lessons to carry forward is the importance of long-term thinking. In a world that often prioritizes quick results, real estate and construction-based strategies require patience and discipline. The rewards are not always immediate, but they are substantial and enduring. Each project you complete adds to your foundation, creating income, equity, and opportunities for future growth. By focusing on the long term, you position yourself to benefit from compounding returns, which is one of the most powerful forces in wealth creation.

Another key takeaway is the importance of control. Owning and developing your own property gives you control over your business environment, your expenses, and your future. Instead of being subject to rent increases or limited by leased space, you create a foundation that supports your growth. This control extends beyond the physical property—it influences your financial decisions, your strategic direction, and your ability to adapt to changing circumstances.

Discipline is the thread that connects every successful project. From maintaining a detailed budget to managing timelines, controlling costs, and making strategic decisions, discipline ensures that your projects stay on track. It also allows you to navigate challenges with confidence, knowing that you have a plan in place. Discipline is not just about avoiding mistakes—it is about consistently doing the right things to achieve your goals.

Relationships are another critical component of success. Throughout your journey, you will work with lenders, contractors, advisors, and partners who play a role in your projects. Building strong, trustworthy relationships creates a network of support that can help you overcome challenges and identify new opportunities. These relationships become more valuable over time, as they are built on experience, trust, and shared success.

Adaptability is equally important. Markets change, conditions evolve, and new opportunities emerge. Being able to adjust your strategy while staying focused on your long-term goals allows you to remain competitive and resilient. This includes staying informed about market trends, exploring new approaches, and continuously improving your processes. Adaptability ensures that your growth is not limited by external factors but driven by your ability to respond effectively.

Another powerful concept is leverage. SBA financing allows you to use a relatively small amount of capital to control a much larger asset. This leverage amplifies your ability to grow, enabling you to achieve results that would not be possible with cash alone. However, leverage must be used wisely. Balancing risk and reward is essential to maintaining financial stability and ensuring that your portfolio continues to perform over time.

As you move forward, it is important to remember that every project is an opportunity to learn and improve. Even the most successful investors encounter challenges, but they use those experiences to refine their approach and become more effective. By embracing a mindset of continuous learning, you can turn every experience into a stepping stone toward greater success.

The concept of legacy should also remain at the forefront of your thinking. The work you do today has the potential to create lasting impact, not only for yourself but for your family and future generations. By building a portfolio of income-producing assets, you create a source of stability and opportunity that extends beyond your lifetime. This is what transforms financial success into true wealth—a system that continues to provide value over time.

It is also worth reflecting on the broader impact of your work. Construction and expansion projects contribute to economic growth, create jobs, and improve communities. By developing properties and businesses, you play a role in shaping the environment around you. This impact adds another dimension to your success, making your work not only financially rewarding but also meaningful.

As you conclude this series, the most important step is to take action. Knowledge without action has no value. The strategies and concepts you have learned are only effective when applied. Start with a clear vision, identify opportunities, and move forward with confidence. Each step you take brings you closer to your goals and strengthens your ability to execute future projects.

The path you are on is one of growth, challenge, and opportunity. It requires commitment, resilience, and a willingness to step outside your comfort zone. But the rewards—financial independence, control over your future, and the ability to create lasting wealth—are well worth the effort.

In the end, SBA construction and expansion financing is not just about building properties—it is about building a life of possibility. It is about turning ideas into reality, creating value where none existed before, and shaping your future with intention and purpose. With the knowledge and strategies you now possess, you are equipped to move forward and create something truly extraordinary.

How to Get a Personalized SBA Commercial Mortgage Review

If you found this book helpful, you may want to see how these strategies apply to your specific financial situation.

SBA commercial mortgage financing is highly customized—your business income, financial statements, credit profile, property type, industry, and long-term goals all play a role in determining what you qualify for and how your loan should be structured.

Every borrower's situation is different. Your revenue trends, business model, tax returns, debt obligations, ownership structure, and the type of commercial property you are purchasing, refinancing, or building all impact your options. The strategies and examples in this book are designed to teach you how SBA commercial mortgage loans work—but your actual loan approval, terms, and structure can only be determined by analyzing your real financial profile.

If you would like a no-obligation SBA Commercial Mortgage review, you can request one here:

Email: info@FinibiMortgage.com

A licensed mortgage broker will review your business financials, income structure, credit profile, and goals, and explain what SBA financing options may be available to you—including:

• SBA 7(a) commercial mortgage loans• SBA 504 fixed-rate commercial real estate financing• Owner-occupied property qualification strategies• Business acquisition with real estate financing• Commercial refinance and cash-out strategies• Construction and expansion loan structuring• Advanced SBA deal structuring to maximize approval

No cost. No pressure. No obligation.

Sincerely,

Joseph G. Correa

Finibi Mortgage Inc.

Licensed Mortgage Broker

About the Author

Joseph G. Correa is a licensed mortgage broker and the founder of Finibi Mortgage, a Florida-based brokerage specializing in SBA commercial mortgage loans, non-QM lending, and strategic real estate financing solutions for business owners, entrepreneurs, and investors.

With more than two decades of experience in mortgage lending, underwriting, and deal structuring, Joseph has helped thousands of clients secure financing for commercial real estate, business acquisitions, and complex transactions using both traditional and alternative lending strategies.

Unlike traditional loan officers who focus only on basic qualification, Joseph's approach emphasizes **cash flow analysis, deal structuring, and strategic financing**. He believes that business owners should not be limited by rigid lending formulas, but instead empowered by understanding how to structure deals that align with lender guidelines and maximize approval potential.

Joseph is widely recognized for his expertise in:

• SBA 7(a) and SBA 504 commercial mortgage loans• Owner-occupied commercial real estate financing• Business acquisition with real estate structuring• Commercial refinance and cash flow optimization• Construction and expansion financing• Advanced loan structuring and approval strategy

Through his education platform, Finibi Academy, Joseph has trained tens of thousands of students worldwide in mortgage strategy, real estate investing, credit optimization, and financial independence.

He created the *SBA Commercial Mortgage Loan Mastery Series* to provide a clear, step-by-step roadmap for borrowers and professionals who want to understand, qualify for, and scale commercial real estate using SBA financing.

His mission is simple:

To help business owners use strategic financing to acquire assets, build cash flow, and create long-term wealth.

When he is not structuring loans or writing, Joseph works with clients across the United States to design customized SBA financing strategies aligned with their business goals and growth plans.

The SBA Commercial Mortgage Loan Mastery Series Roadmap

The Complete Guide to Using SBA Financing to Build Commercial Real Estate and Business Wealth

The purpose of *The SBA Commercial Mortgage Loan Mastery Series* is to give business owners, investors, and mortgage professionals the exact strategies used by lenders and underwriters—translated into simple, practical steps you can apply in real life.

This series takes you from beginner to advanced mastery of how to qualify, structure, and scale commercial real estate and business financing using SBA mortgage loans.

Each book builds on the last. You are not just learning how to get approved—you are learning how to control your approvals and scale your opportunities.

Book 1 — SBA Commercial Mortgage Loan Fundamentals Understand how SBA mortgage programs work, including 7(a) and 504 loans, and how to qualify.

Book 2 — Getting Approved for an SBA Commercial Mortgage Loan Learn step-by-step strategies to meet lender requirements and secure funding.

Book 3 — Owner-Occupied Property Financing with SBA Loans Learn how to buy or refinance your business property using SBA financing.

Book 4 — Buying a Business and Real Estate with SBA Financing Acquire a business and its property in one structured transaction.

Book 5 — SBA 7(a) Mortgage Loan Strategies Master flexible loan structures for business and real estate funding.

Book 6 — SBA 504 Mortgage Loans for Commercial Real Estate Use long-term fixed-rate financing for large property acquisitions.

Book 7 — Refinancing Commercial Debt with SBA Loans Lower payments, improve cash flow, and restructure existing debt.

Book 8 — SBA Loans for Construction and Expansion Build, renovate, and scale commercial properties with structured financing.

Book 9 — SBA Loan Requirements, Rates, and Structures Understand how to compare options and choose the best loan.

Book 10 — Advanced SBA Commercial Mortgage Structuring Engineer approvals and maximize leverage using expert strategies.

This series is designed to move you from:

Understanding → Execution → Scaling → Mastery

By the end, you will not just know how to qualify—you will know how to structure, analyze, and scale deals like a professional.

Educational & Financial Disclaimer

The *SBA Commercial Mortgage Loan Mastery Series* is intended for educational and informational purposes only.

This content is designed to help readers understand SBA commercial mortgage lending, real estate financing strategies, and business acquisition concepts. It is not financial, legal, tax, or investment advice.

Joseph G. Correa and Live Stronger Faster are not acting as your personal financial advisor, attorney, accountant, or mortgage professional through this publication.

SBA loan programs, underwriting guidelines, interest rates, and lender requirements may change at any time and vary by lender.

All examples in this series are for illustration purposes only and do not guarantee approval or results.

Always consult with licensed professionals before making financial decisions.

Risk Disclosure

SBA commercial mortgage lending and real estate investing involve risk.

Business performance, income stability, interest rate changes, market conditions, and lender guidelines can all impact loan approval and financial outcomes.

Borrowing against real estate or using leverage increases both potential returns and risk.

Failure to repay a loan may result in foreclosure and loss of property.

Cash flow, rental income, appreciation, and business performance are not guaranteed.

All strategies presented in this series are educational and must be evaluated based on your individual financial situation.

You are solely responsible for your financial decisions.